A BALANCED MATHEMATICS PROGRAM INTEGRATING SCIENCE AND LANGUAGE ARTS

Unit Resource Guide
Unit 14
Collecting
and Using Data

THIRD EDITION

KENDALL/HUNT PUBLISHING COMPANY
4050 Westmark Drive   Dubuque, Iowa 52002

A TIMS® Curriculum
University of Illinois at Chicago

UIC The University of Illinois
at Chicago

The original edition was based on work supported by the National Science Foundation under grant
No. MDR 9050226 and the University of Illinois at Chicago. Any opinions, findings, and conclusions
or recommendations expressed in this publication are those of the author(s) and do not necessarily
reflect the views of the granting agencies.

Letter Home

Collecting and Using Data

Date: _____

Dear Family Member:

During this unit our class will collect data and use it to make predictions and solve problems. For one activity, students work in groups to gather survey data about the other students in the room. Another activity is a long-term project that continues for two or more weeks. Each student will record the number of minutes and the number of pages he or she reads each day. Students keep track of the total number of minutes and pages read by the entire class. Your child will bring home a data table similar to the one shown below. Your help in filling out the table and encouraging your child to read at home will contribute to the success of the project.

My Tracking Our Reading Data

Title	Date	Number of Pages	Beginning Time	Ending Time	Number of Minutes	Adult's Initials for Reading at Home	
The Ghostly Galleons	3-6-07	8	10:00 A.M.	10:20 A.M.	20		
Reptiles	3-6-07	2	8:36 P.M.	8:50 P.M.	15	CRK	

To help students collect the reading data, the class will learn to tell time to the nearest minute using clocks that have hands and numbers. Encourage your child to tell time using these clocks rather than digital clocks. We call these analog clocks. If you do not have such a clock in your house, you may wish to consider buying an inexpensive watch with hands and numbers or an alarm clock for your child's room.

Math Facts. Help your child learn the multiplication facts for the nines using the *Triangle Flash Cards*.

Thank you for taking time to support at home what we do in school.

Sincerely,

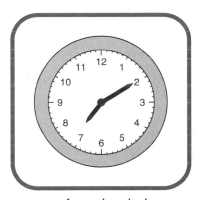

An analog clock

Carta al hogar

Recolectando y usando datos

Fecha: _____

Estimado miembro de familia:

En esta unidad, la clase recolectará datos y los usará para hacer predicciones y resolver problemas. En una actividad, los estudiantes trabajarán en grupos para recolectar datos para una encuesta sobre los demás estudiantes de la clase. Otra actividad es un proyecto a largo plazo que durará dos o más semanas. Cada estudiantes registrará el número de minutos y el número de páginas que lee por día. Los estudiantes llevarán un registro del número total de minutos y páginas que lee toda la clase. Su hijo/a llevará a casa una tabla de datos similar a la que aparece en la ilustración. Su ayuda para llenar la tabla y animar a su hijo/a a leer en casa contribuirá al éxito del proyecto.

Registro de lectura

Título	Fecha	Número de páginas	Hora de comienzo	Hora de finalización	Número de minutos	Iniciales de un adulto para la lectura en casa	
Los galeones fantasmales	3-6-04	8	10:00 A.M.	10:20 A.M.	20		
Reptiles	3-6-04	2	8:36 P.M.	8:50 P.M.	15	CRK	

Para ayudar a los estudiantes a recolectar los datos sobre lectura, la clase aprenderá a decir la hora redondeando al minuto más cercano usando relojes que tienen manecillas y números. Anime a su hijo/a a decir la hora usando estos relojes digitales. Estos relojes se llaman en lugar de relojes análogos. Si no tiene uno de estos relojes en su casa, sería una buena idea comprar un reloj barato con manecillas y números o un reloj despertador para la habitación de su hijo/a.

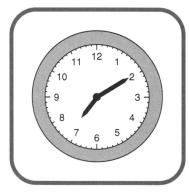

Un reloj análogo

- **Conceptos básicos.** Ayude a su hijo/a a aprender la tabla de multiplicación del nueve usando las tarjetas triangulares.

Gracias por tomarse el tiempo para ayudar en casa con lo que hacemos en la escuela.

Atentamente,

Table of Contents

Unit 14
Collecting and Using Data

Unit 14

Outline
Collecting and Using Data

Unit Summary

Estimated Class Sessions
7-10

A major objective of this unit is to give students more autonomy as they work on a lab and solve problems. In the lab *Make Your Own Survey,* students work with a group to conduct a survey using the TIMS Laboratory Method. With as little assistance as possible, they choose a variable to study and then organize, collect, display, and analyze the data. The class also works cooperatively to plan and implement a "reading drive" by setting goals for the amount of reading they will do over a given period of time. They keep track of their reading by collecting and displaying the data. The data provides a context for problem solving using addition and subtraction of larger numbers, reading a clock to the nearest minute, and finding elapsed time. The DPP for this unit provides practice with and assesses the multiplication facts for the nines.

Major Concept Focus

- telling time to the nearest minute
- elapsed time
- Game: telling time on digital and analog clocks
- simple percentages as benchmarks
- TIMS Laboratory Method
- bar graphs
- importance of accurate data
- surveys
- multidigit addition
- multidigit subtraction
- addition algorithms
- subtraction algorithms
- variables and values
- practice and assessment of the multiplication facts for the 9s

Pacing Suggestions

- Lesson 3 *Tracking Our Reading* begins a long-term project that will take two to three weeks to complete. Setting up the investigation will take one day. Then students collect data over a two- or three-week period. The class will need another class session to analyze the collected data.
- In Lesson 5 *Reviewing Addition and Subtraction* students review using base-ten pieces, mental math strategies, and paper and pencil to add and subtract multidigit numbers. Students' abilities with these skills will determine the number of days students will need to solve the problems.

Assessment Indicators

Use the following Assessment Indicators and the *Observational Assessment Record* that follows the Background section in this unit to assess students on key ideas.

A1. Can students tell time to the nearest minute?

A2. Can students solve problems involving elapsed time?

A3. Can students collect, organize, graph, and analyze data?

A4. Can students make and interpret bar graphs?

A5. Can students identify and use variables in a survey?

A6. Can students add and subtract multidigit numbers using paper and pencil?

A7. Can students solve problems involving addition and subtraction?

A8. Do students demonstrate fluency with the multiplication facts for the 9s?

Unit Planner

KEY: SG = Student Guide, DAB = Discovery Assignment Book, AB = Adventure Book, URG = Unit Resource Guide, DPP = Daily Practice and Problems, HP = Home Practice (found in Discovery Assignment Book), and TIG = Teacher Implementation Guide.

	Lesson Information	Supplies	Copies/Transparencies

Lesson 1

Time Again

URG Pages 19–33
SG Pages 194–200

DPP A–B
HP Part 1

Estimated Class Sessions
1

Activity
Students practice telling time to the nearest minute. They take part in various 5-minute activities, e.g., reading, practicing subtraction facts, listening to music. They note the time on an analog clock before and after each activity. They also practice finding elapsed time.

Math Facts
DPP Bit A reminds students to practice the multiplication facts using the *Triangle Flash Cards: 9s*.

Homework
1. Assign as homework any problems not used in class on the *Time Again* Activity Pages.
2. Assign Part 1 of the Home Practice.
3. Remind students to take home their *Triangle Flash Cards* to study with a family member.

Assessment
1. Students complete the *More Time* Assessment Blackline Master.
2. Use the *Observational Assessment Record* to document students' abilities to tell time to the nearest minute and to solve problems involving elapsed time.

Supplies:
- analog demonstration clock
- 1 pair of scissors per student
- 1 brad per student
- 1 envelope for storing flash cards per student
- things to do for 5 minutes such as read a book or *Triangle Flash Cards*, optional
- 1 clear jar with straight sides (e.g., small peanut butter jar) for each water clock (extension) per student, optional
- 1 large plastic jug with a cap (e.g., milk or soda bottle) for each water clock (extension) per student, optional
- masking tape (extension), optional
- food coloring (extension), optional
- small nail (extension), optional
- hammer (extension), optional

Copies/Transparencies:
- 1 copy of *Clock* URG Page 29 on card stock per student, optional
- 1 copy of *More Time* URG Page 30 per student
- 1 copy of *Observational Assessment Record* URG Pages 9–10 to be used throughout this unit

Lesson 2

Time and Time Again

URG Pages 34–40
SG Page 201
DAB Pages 221–227

DPP C–D
HP Part 2

Estimated Class Sessions
1

Game
Students play a variation of the card games *Concentration* and *Lotto*, in which players find pairs from memory. In this game, players turn over face-down cards, seeking to match the time on an analog clock to the corresponding digital time.

Math Facts
DPP Bit C provides practice with the multiplication facts for the 9s. Task D provides practice with the nines and multiples of ten.

Homework
1. Students take the cards home to play the game with a family member.
2. Assign Part 2 of the Home Practice.

Supplies:
- 1 pair of scissors per student

	Lesson Information	Supplies	Copies/ Transparencies
Lesson 3 **Tracking Our Reading** URG Pages 41–54 SG Page 202 DPP E–F HP Part 3 *Estimated Class Sessions* **1-2**	**Activity** This lesson is the beginning of a long-term class project that will continue for two or more weeks. During the first week, the class collects data on students' reading and uses the data to set a goal for the following week or two. The class continues to collect more data to see if they can meet their goal. **Math Facts** DPP Bit E provides practice with multiplication facts. **Homework** 1. Students will read at home and record their data. 2. Assign Part 3 of the Home Practice.	• large sheet of paper or a flip chart for recording class data	• 2 copies of *Eight-column Data Table* URG Page 53 per student, optional • 1 enlarged (and laminated) copy of *Reading Goal Scale* URG Page 52 for the class or 100 cc graduated cylinder and colored water
Lesson 4 **Make Your Own Survey** URG Pages 55–71 SG Pages 203–208 DPP G–J HP Part 4 *Estimated Class Sessions* **2-3**	**Lab** Students work in groups to gather survey data about the other students in the room. Students independently choose a variable to study. They investigate, collect and organize data, and present their findings to the class. The importance of reporting data accurately and honestly is discussed. **Math Facts** DPP Bit G is the Multiplication Quiz: 9s. Task J reviews square numbers. **Homework** 1. Students bring examples of survey data from newspapers or magazines. 2. Assign Part 4 of the Home Practice. **Assessment** 1. Assign scores to students' surveys and record comments on their performance using the *TIMS Laboratory Method Checklist* and the *TIMS Multidimensional Rubric*. 2. Use DPP Bit G to assess students' fluency with the multiplication facts for the nines.	• 1 class names list per student group	• 1–2 copies of *Centimeter Graph Paper* URG Page 65 per student • 1 *Three-column, Four-column, Five-column,* or *Eight-column Data Table* URG Pages 53 & 66–68 per student as selected • 1 *TIMS Laboratory Method Checklist* URG Page 64 per student pair for assessment, optional • 1 transparency of *Three-column Data Table* URG Page 66, optional • 1 transparency of *Centimeter Graph Paper* URG Page 65, optional • 1 copy of *TIMS Multidimensional Rubric* TIG, Assessment section
Lesson 5 **Reviewing Addition and Subtraction** URG Pages 72–85 SG Pages 209–215 DPP K–N *Estimated Class Sessions* **2-3**	**Activity** Students review adding and subtracting large numbers using base-ten pieces and pencil and paper. Using the data from *Tracking Our Reading* as a context, students solve problems involving addition and subtraction. **Homework** Assign the Homework section on the *Reviewing Addition and Subtraction* Activity Pages. **Assessment** 1. Students complete the *Addition and Subtraction* Assessment Blackline Master.	• 1 set of base-ten pieces (2 packs, 14 flats, 30 skinnies, and 50 bits) per student and 1 set for the teacher • magnetic base-ten pieces and a magnetic board or overhead base-ten pieces, optional	• 1 copy of *Addition and Subtraction* URG Pages 80–81 per student • 1 copy of *Individual Assessment Record Sheet* TIG Assessment section per student, previously copied for use throughout the year

(Continued)

Lesson Information	Supplies	Copies/ Transparencies
2. Use the *Observational Assessment Record* to note students' abilities to represent multidigit addition and subtraction problems using base-ten pieces. 3. Transfer appropriate documentation from the Unit 14 *Observational Assessment Record* to the students' *Individual Assessment Record Sheets*.		

Connections

A current list of literature and software connections is available at *www.mathtrailblazers.com*. You can also find information on connections in the *Teacher Implementation Guide* Literature List and Software List sections.

Literature Connections

Suggested Titles

- Hutchins, Pat. *Clocks and More Clocks*. Aladdin Paperbacks, Hong Kong, 1994. (Lesson 1)
- Murphy, Stuart J. *Get Up and Go!* Harper Collins Publishers, New York, 1996.
- Nagda, Ann Whitehead and Bickel, Cindy. *Tiger Math: Learning to Graph From a Baby Tiger.* Henry Holt and Company, New York, 2000.

Software Connections

- *Discover Time* provides practice in telling time to the nearest hour, half-hour, quarter hour, and five-minute intervals.
- *Graphers* is a data graphing tool appropriate for young students.
- *Kid Pix* allows students to create their own illustrations.
- *Math Arena* is a collection of math activities that reinforces many math concepts.
- *Mighty Math Calculating Crew* poses short-answer questions about number operations and money skills.
- *National Library of Virtual Manipulatives* website (http://matti.usu.edu) allows students to work with manipulatives including base-ten pieces, the abacus, and many others.
- *Tabletop Jr.* provides students the opportunity to work with data and develops logical thinking.

Teaching All Math Trailblazers Students

Math Trailblazers® lessons are designed for students with a wide range of abilities. The lessons are flexible and do not require significant adaptation for diverse learning styles or academic levels. However, when needed, lessons can be tailored to allow students to engage their abilities to the greatest extent possible while building knowledge and skills.

To assist you in meeting the needs of all students in your classroom, this section contains information about some of the features in the curriculum that allow all students access to mathematics. For additional information, see the Teaching the *Math Trailblazers* Student: Meeting Individual Needs section in the *Teacher Implementation Guide*.

Differentiation Opportunities in this Unit

Games

Use games to promote or extend understanding of math concepts and to practice skills with children who need more practice.

- Lesson 2 *Time and Time Again*

Laboratory Experiments

Laboratory experiments enable students to solve problems using a variety of representations including pictures, tables, graphs, and symbols. Teachers can assign or adapt parts of the analysis according to the student's ability. The following lesson is a lab:

- Lesson 4 *Make Your Own Survey*

Journal Prompts

Journal prompts provide opportunities for students to explain and reflect on mathematical problems. They can help both students who need practice explaining their ideas and students who benefit from answering higher order questions. Students with various learning styles can express themselves using pictures, words, and sentences. Teachers can alter journal prompts to suit students' ability levels. The following lessons contain a journal prompt:

- Lesson 1 *Time Again*
- Lesson 2 *Time and Time Again*

- Lesson 3 *Tracking Our Reading*
- Lesson 4 *Make Your Own Survey*
- Lesson 5 *Reviewing Addition and Subtraction*

DPP Challenges

DPP Challenges are items from the Daily Practice and Problems that usually take more than fifteen minutes to complete. These problems are more thought-provoking and can be used to stretch students' problem-solving skills. The following lesson has a DPP Challenge in it:

- DPP Challenge N from Lesson 5 *Reviewing Addition and Subtraction*

Extensions

Use extensions to enrich lessons. Many extensions provide opportunities to further involve or challenge students of all abilities. Take a moment to review the extensions prior to beginning this unit. Some extensions may require additional preparation and planning. The following lessons contain extensions:

- Lesson 1 *Time Again*
- Lesson 3 *Tracking Our Reading*
- Lesson 4 *Make Your Own Survey*

Background
Collecting and Using Data

A major objective of this unit is to give students more autonomy as they work on a lab and solve problems. In the beginning of the year, students were provided with a great deal of structure while working on labs. For example, in the two labs in Unit 1 *Sampling and Classifying*, the variable to be studied was chosen for students, data tables with column headings were provided, and the graph paper already had the axes labeled and scaled. Students analyzed the data as part of a teacher-led discussion. As the year progressed, students were expected to become more independent. As part of a small group, they decided how to label the column headings in data tables, scale and label the axes on graphs, and use their data to solve problems.

In this unit students work with a group to conduct a survey using the TIMS Laboratory Method. With as little assistance as possible, they will choose a variable to study and then organize, collect, display, and analyze the data. For more information regarding the TIMS Laboratory Method, refer to the TIMS Tutor: *The TIMS Laboratory Method* in the *Teacher Implementation Guide*.

Another goal of this unit is to collect data that will provide a context for extending and reviewing skills and concepts previously studied. Students collect data on the amount of reading they do in the *Tracking Our Reading* activity. To collect this data, students must know how to read a clock and find elapsed time. The data, which includes the number of minutes and pages read, also provides a context for the class to solve many problems. The class reviews multidigit addition and subtraction using the base-ten pieces. As they work on problems, they increase their proficiency using pencil-and-paper procedures.

Resources

- Goudsmit, Samuel A., Robert Claiborne, and the Editors of Time-Life Books. *Time*. Time-Life Books, New York, 1966.
- Zubrowski, Bernie. *Clocks: Building and Experimenting with Model Timepieces*. Morrow Junior Books, New York, 1988.

Observational Assessment Record

(A1) Can students tell time to the nearest minute?

(A2) Can students solve problems involving elapsed time?

(A3) Can students collect, organize, graph, and analyze data?

(A4) Can students make and interpret bar graphs?

(A5) Can students identify and use variables in a survey?

(A6) Can students add and subtract multidigit numbers using paper and pencil?

(A7) Can students solve problems involving addition and subtraction?

(A8) Do students demonstrate fluency with the multiplication facts for the 9s?

(A9) _____

Name	A1	A2	A3	A4	A5	A6	A7	A8	A9	Comments
1.										
2.										
3.										
4.										
5.										
6.										
7.										
8.										
9.										
10.										
11.										
12.										
13.										

Name	A1	A2	A3	A4	A5	A6	A7	A8	A9	Comments
14.										
15.										
16.										
17.										
18.										
19.										
20.										
21.										
22.										
23.										
24.										
25.										
26.										
27.										
28.										
29.										
30.										
31.										
32.										

Unit 14

Daily Practice and Problems
Collecting and Using Data

A DPP Menu for Unit 14

Two Daily Practice and Problems (DPP) items are included for each class session listed in the Unit Outline. A scope and sequence chart for the DPP is in the *Teacher Implementation Guide*.

Icons in the Teacher Notes column designate the subject matter of each DPP item. The first item in each class session is always a Bit and the second is either a Task or Challenge. Each item falls into one or more of the categories listed below. A menu of the DPP items for Unit 14 follows.

N Number Sense	X Computation	Time	Geometry
D, F, H, L	D, J, N	B, I, K, M	F, J

5×7 Math Facts	$ Money	Measurement	Data
A, C–E, G, J		F	I, K, M

Practicing and Assessing the Multiplication Facts

In Unit 11, students began the systematic, strategies-based study of the multiplication facts. In this unit, students practice and are assessed on the multiplication facts for the nines. The *Triangle Flash Cards: 9s* can be found in the *Discovery Assignment Book* immediately following the Home Practice. In Unit 14, DPP items A, C, D, and E provide practice with multiplication facts for the nines. Bit G is the Multiplication Quiz: 9s.

For information on the distribution and study of the multiplication facts in Grade 3, see the Daily Practice and Problems Guides for Units 3 and 11. For a detailed explanation of our approach to learning and assessing the math facts in Grade 3 see the *Grade 3 Facts Resource Guide* and for information for Grades K–5, see the TIMS Tutor: *Math Facts* in the *Teacher Implementation Guide*.

Students may solve the items individually, in groups, or as a class. The items may also be assigned for homework. The DPPs are also available on the Teacher Resource CD.

Student Questions	Teacher Notes

 Triangle Flash Cards: 9s

With a partner, use your *Triangle Flash Cards* to quiz each other on the multiplication facts for the nines. One partner covers the corner containing the highest number. The second person multiplies the two uncovered numbers.

Separate the used cards into three piles: those facts you know and can answer quickly, those you can figure out with a strategy, and those you need to learn. Practice the last two piles again and then, for homework, make a list of the facts you need to practice at home.

Circle the facts you know quickly on your *Multiplication Facts I Know* chart.

TIMS Bit

The *Triangle Flash Cards* follow the Home Practice in the *Discovery Assignment Book*. They should be sent home for practice.

Have students record the facts they know well on their *Multiplication Facts I Know* charts. Students should circle the facts they know and can answer quickly. Since these charts can also be used as multiplication tables, students should have them available to use as needed.

Inform students when you will give the quiz on the nines. This quiz appears in DPP Bit G.

Student Questions	Teacher Notes

 B **Five More Minutes**

TIMS Task

1. Tino was five minutes early for his 9:30 dentist appointment. What time did he arrive?

1. 9:25

2. 10:50

3. 5 patients (9:30, 9:45, 10:00, 10:15, 10:30)

2. Tina was five minutes late for her 10:45 appointment. What time did she arrive?

3. Their dentist schedules appointments 15 minutes apart. How many patients are scheduled to see the dentist between 9:30 and 10:45?

C **Triples**

TIMS Bit

1. A. $3 \times 2 =$
   B. $3 \times 3 \times 2 =$
   C. $9 \times 2 =$

1. A. 6
   B. 18
   C. 18

2. A. $3 \times 3 =$
   B. $3 \times 3 \times 3 =$
   C. $9 \times 3 =$

2. A. 9
   B. 27
   C. 27

3. A. $3 \times 4 =$
   B. $3 \times 3 \times 4 =$
   C. $9 \times 4 =$

3. A. 12
   B. 36
   C. 36

4. A. $3 \times 5 =$
   B. $3 \times 3 \times 5 =$
   C. $9 \times 5 =$

4. A. 15
   B. 45
   C. 45

Encourage students to describe any patterns they see.

Multiples of 10 and 100

Use the patterns you found in your multiplication table for multiplying by 10 and 100 to do the following problems.

1. $2 \times 9 =$

2. $2 \times 90 =$

3. $2 \times 900 =$

4. $9 \times 7 =$

5. $9 \times 70 =$

6. $9 \times 700 =$

7. $4 \times 9 =$

8. $4 \times 90 =$

9. $4 \times 900 =$

TIMS Task

1. 18   2. 180

3. 1800   4. 63

5. 630   6. 6300

7. 36   8. 360

9. 3600

E **Fine Nines**

Do these problems in your head. Write only the answers.

A. $9 \times 1 =$

B. $9 \times 7 =$

C. $8 \times 9 =$

D. $9 \times 2 =$

E. $6 \times 9 =$

F. $9 \times 4 =$

G. $10 \times 9 =$

H. $9 \times 9 =$

I. $9 \times 3 =$

J. $5 \times 9 =$

K. $9 \times 0 =$

TIMS Bit

Ask students what strategies they use to solve these problems. One possible strategy for finding nine times a number is to multiply the number by ten, then subtract the number from the total. (Example: $9 \times 6 = 10 \times 6 - 6$)

A. 9   B. 63

C. 72   D. 18

E. 54   F. 36

G. 90   H. 81

I. 27   J. 45

K. 0

Six-tenths

Draw a rectangle 5 cm long and 4 cm wide. Divide the rectangle into ten equal parts. Color six of the parts.

1. Write a fraction for the shaded area of the rectangle.

2. Write a fraction for the unshaded area.

TIMS Task

Distribute *Centimeter Grid Paper.*

The most common solutions are:

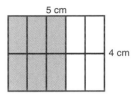

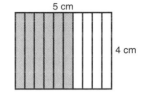

1. $\frac{6}{10}$ 2. $\frac{4}{10}$

 Multiplication Quiz: 9s

A. $3 \times 9 =$ B. $9 \times 7 =$

C. $10 \times 9 =$ D. $0 \times 9 =$

E. $5 \times 9 =$ F. $9 \times 8 =$

G. $6 \times 9 =$ H. $4 \times 9 =$

I. $9 \times 9 =$ J. $9 \times 2 =$

K. $9 \times 1 =$

TIMS Bit

This quiz is on the fourth group of multiplication facts, the nines. We recommend 2 minutes for this quiz. Allow students to change pens after the time is up and complete the remaining problems in a different color.

After students take the test, have them update their *Multiplication Facts I Know* charts.

A. 27	B. 63
C. 90	D. 0
E. 45	F. 72
G. 54	H. 36
I. 81	J. 18
K. 9	

H Some Percents

What is 50% of

A. 20?   B. 40?

C. 17?   D. 1000?

What is 25% of

E. 20?   F. 40?

G. 17?   H. 1000?

TIMS Task

A. 10   B. 20

C. $8\frac{1}{2}$ D. 500

E. 5   F. 10

G. $4\frac{1}{4}$ H. 250

I Tracking Our Reading 1

Record your reading data the way your class decided.

TIMS Bit

The remaining bits in this unit will remind students to record their reading data. This ongoing activity was introduced in Unit 14 Lesson 3. Change the wording depending on what the class decided. Include "don't forgets" that match class decisions.

J Square Numbers

1. What square number is shown by all the small squares below?

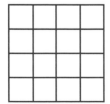

2. What other square numbers do you see?

3. Bob thinks 8 is a square number. Show him why it is not.

TIMS Task

1. 16

2. 1, 4, and 9

3. 4 is 2 × 2 and 9 is 3 × 3. So, there are no square numbers between 4 and 9.

Tracking Our Reading 2

Record your reading data the way your class decided.

TIMS Bit

The remaining bits in this unit will remind students to record their reading data. This ongoing activity was introduced in Unit 14 Lesson 3. Change the wording depending on what the class decided. Include "don't forgets" that match class decisions.

 Counting by Thirds

Skip count by thirds backwards from 10.

$\frac{1}{3}$	$\frac{1}{3}$	$\frac{1}{3}$	$\frac{1}{3}$	$\frac{1}{3}$	$\frac{1}{3}$	$\frac{1}{3}$

10    $9\frac{2}{3}$ $9\frac{1}{3}$ 9 $8\frac{2}{3}$ $8\frac{1}{3}$ 8 $7\frac{2}{3}$

TIMS Task

Students can use the diagram to help them start counting backwards by thirds.

 Tracking Our Reading 3

Record your reading data the way your class decided.

TIMS Bit

Remind students to record their reading data. This ongoing activity was introduced in Unit 14 Lesson 3. Change the wording depending on what the class decided. Include "don't forgets" that match class decisions.

Adding and Subtracting

Solve the following problems on a sheet of paper. Use base-ten pieces or base-ten shorthand if it helps. Estimate to be sure your answers are reasonable.

1. $\begin{array}{r} 137 \\ + 446 \\ \hline \end{array}$

2. $\begin{array}{r} 439 \\ - 176 \\ \hline \end{array}$

3. $\begin{array}{r} 2348 \\ + 4769 \\ \hline \end{array}$

4. $\begin{array}{r} 504 \\ - 426 \\ \hline \end{array}$

5. Explain your estimation strategy for Question 3.

6. Explain how to do Question 4 using mental math.

TIMS Challenge

1. 583

2. 263

3. 7117

4. 78

5. Possible strategy:
   2300 + 4700 = 2000 + 4000 + 1000 = 7000.

6. Possible strategy: Count up from 426 using 25 as a convenient number. 425 to 500 is 75. One less is 74 + 4 is 78.

Lesson 1

Time Again

Lesson Overview

Estimated Class Sessions

1

Students practice telling time to the nearest minute. They also solve problems involving elapsed time so they will be able to record the amount of time they read each day in Lesson 3 *Tracking Our Reading*. In an extension activity, students make a simple water clock.

Key Content

- Telling time to the nearest minute.
- Solving problems involving elapsed time.

Math Facts

DPP Bit A reminds students to practice the multiplication facts using the *Triangle Flash Cards: 9s*.

Homework

1. Assign as homework any problems not used in class on the *Time Again* Activity Pages.
2. Assign Part 1 of the Home Practice.
3. Remind students to take home their *Triangle Flash Cards* to study with a family member.

Assessment

1. Students complete the *More Time* Assessment Blackline Master.
2. Use the *Observational Assessment Record* to document students' abilities to tell time to the nearest minute and to solve problems involving elapsed time.

Curriculum Sequence

Before This Unit

Telling Time

Students practiced telling time to the nearest five minutes in Grade 3 Unit 4 Lesson 5 *It's Time* and solved problems involving elapsed time in Lesson 6 *Time for Problems*.

After This Unit

Telling Time

Students will practice telling time and solving problems about elapsed time in the Daily Practice and Problems in succeeding units.

Materials List

Supplies and Copies

Student	Teacher
Supplies for Each Student	**Supplies**
• scissors • brad • envelope for storing flash cards • things to do for 5 minutes such as read a book or practice *Triangle Flash Cards,* optional • clear jar with straight sides (e.g., small peanut butter jar) for each water clock (extension), optional • large plastic jug with a cap (e.g., milk or soda bottle) for each water clock (extension), optional • masking tape (extension), optional • food coloring (extension), optional	• analog demonstration clock • small nail (extension), optional • hammer (extension), optional
Copies	**Copies/Transparencies**
• 1 copy of *Clock* on card stock per student, optional (*Unit Resource Guide* Page 29) • 1 copy of *More Time* per student (*Unit Resource Guide* Page 30)	• 1 copy of *Observational Assessment Record* to be used throughout this unit (*Unit Resource Guide* Pages 9–10)

All blackline masters including assessment, transparency, and DPP masters are also on the Teacher Resource CD.

Student Books
Time Again (*Student Guide* Pages 194–200)
Triangle Flash Cards: 9s (*Discovery Assignment Book* Page 219)

Daily Practice and Problems and Home Practice
DPP items A–B (*Unit Resource Guide* Pages 12–13)
Home Practice Part 1 (*Discovery Assignment Book* Page 216)

Note: Classrooms whose pacing differs significantly from the suggested pacing of the units should use the Math Facts Calendar in Section 4 of the *Facts Resource Guide* to ensure students receive the complete math facts program.

Assessment Tools
Observational Assessment Record (*Unit Resource Guide* Pages 9–10)

Daily Practice and Problems

Suggestions for using the DPPs are on page 27.

A. Bit: Triangle Flash Cards: 9s
(URG p. 12)

With a partner, use your *Triangle Flash Cards* to quiz each other on the multiplication facts for the nines. One partner covers the corner containing the highest number. The second person multiplies the two uncovered numbers.

Separate the used cards into three piles: those facts you know and can answer quickly, those you can figure out with a strategy, and those you need to learn. Practice the last two piles again and then, for homework, make a list of the facts you need to practice at home.

Circle the facts you know quickly on your *Multiplication Facts I Know* chart.

B. Task: Five More Minutes (URG p. 13)

1. Tino was five minutes early for his 9:30 dentist appointment. What time did he arrive?
2. Tina was five minutes late for her 10:45 appointment. What time did she arrive?
3. Their dentist schedules appointments 15 minutes apart. How many patients are scheduled to see the dentist between 9:30 and 10:45?

Part 1 Telling Time to the Minute

The *Time Again* Activity Pages in the *Student Guide* present a brief history of clocks and offer an extension of building a water clock.

To begin the activity, review the position of the hour and minute hand for various times of the day. At first, keep your minutes to multiples of five. Point out the five minute tick marks on your demonstration clock and ask students to skip count by fives as you point to each mark.

Students may make their own clocks using the *Clock* Blackline Master or they may follow along as you model times on the demonstration clock. Encourage students to tell modeled times and then ask them to model specific times for you.

Continue to ask students to show the positions of the hour and minute hand for other times that are 5-minute multiples until you feel they are ready to discuss telling time to the nearest minute.

Time Again

There are many kinds of clocks. Before mechanical clocks were invented, people around the world told time in different ways. One of the earliest clocks in ancient Egypt used the shadows cast by the sun.

At first, people used a shadow clock. This clock had to be turned toward the east in the morning and toward the west in the afternoon. Later, the sundial was developed. Sundials use a round face and the shadow of a tall object to tell the time. Sundials were used in Egypt, India, Babylonia, China, Greece, and many other places.

People still use sundials as decorations in gardens. When can you use a sundial?

In early China and Greece, people used water clocks to tell time. Ancient people in many other parts of the world also used water clocks. In a water clock, water flows from one pot into another pot or pots. A device inside the bottom jar—either a scale or a float—shows the time according to the amount of water in the jar.

Student Guide - page 194

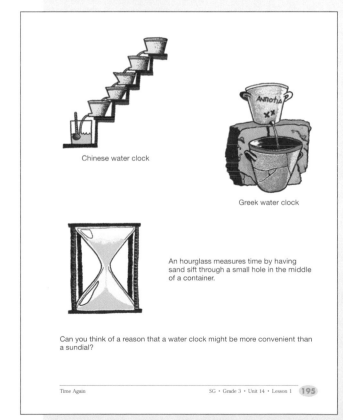

Chinese water clock

Greek water clock

An hourglass measures time by having sand sift through a small hole in the middle of a container.

Can you think of a reason that a water clock might be more convenient than a sundial?

Student Guide - page 195

Discuss

Write the time shown on each clock.

1.

2.

3.

4.

5.

6.

7.

8.

9.

196   SG • Grade 3 • Unit 14 • Lesson 1   Time Again

Student Guide - page 196 (Answers on p. 31)

Journal Prompt

The time is 11:26. Why isn't the hour hand pointing to the 11?

At this point, ask students to look at *Questions 1–3* on the *Time Again* Activity Pages.

Ask:

- *About what time is it in Question 1?* (about 10:00)
- *Is the minute hand pointing exactly to the hour?* (no)
- *Where is the minute hand pointing?* (just a little to the right of the hour, two tick marks)
- *How many minutes are in one hour?* (60 minutes)
- *Where would the minute hand be to show five minutes past ten o'clock?* (at the one)
- *So, if the minute hand is two tick marks past the hour, what time is it exactly?* (2 minutes past ten o'clock or 10:02)

Practice telling time to the minute using *Questions 1–9.* Observe your students' skills and abilities to tell these times.

24   URG • Grade 3 • Unit 14 • Lesson 1

Part 2 Elapsed Time

Students practice finding elapsed times with the *Time Again* Activity Pages. *Questions 10–19* provide elapsed time problems in three different styles. Students are challenged to find the elapsed times when the start and end times are given in *Questions 10–13* and in *Questions 18–19*. *Questions 14–15* give the start time and duration and students must find the end times. *Questions 16–17* give the end time and duration. Students must find the start times.

Prepare your students for work with elapsed time by reading and discussing the sample problem preceding *Question 10*. Discuss the two strategies used to solve the problem. Then, ask students if there are other ways to solve the problem. Students may suggest skip counting by tens or fifteens, adding whole hours then minutes, or modeling the elapsed time on a student clock and counting the time as it passes. Model each of the strategies on the demonstration clock and discuss their effectiveness.

Students often find *Questions 14–15* challenging, so it is important to discuss these problems. Students must first tell how long a time is in minutes and hours, then tell the end time. They may be confused when they see elapsed time written as 130 minutes. Many students think this means one hour and 30 minutes instead of 2 hours and 10 minutes. Provide additional practice for converting times from minutes to hours and vice versa before completing these problems. Continue to work on elapsed time problems as a class. Work through one or two of each type of problem on the activity pages. Encourage students to share and discuss their strategies.

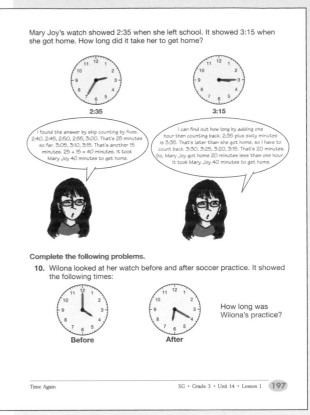

Student Guide - page 197 (Answers on p. 31)

11. Seth looked at his watch before and after gymnastics. It showed the following times:

How long was Seth's gymnastics practice?

12. Lance went to the store for groceries. He left his apartment at 4:15. He returned home at 4:50. How long did it take Lance to get groceries?

13. Polly went to the park at 10:30 A.M. She returned home at 1:25 P.M. How long was Polly at the park?

14. Rodrigo said it took him 90 minutes to do his homework.
    A. How long is 90 minutes in hours and minutes?
    B. If Rodrigo started his homework at 4:15, what time did he finish?

15. Meghan said it took her 130 minutes to do her homework.
    A. How long is 130 minutes in hours and minutes?
    B. If Meghan started her homework at 3:30, what time did she finish?

16. Sherry's watch shows 3:10. What time was it one hour and 5 minutes ago?

17. Dana's watch shows 5:40. What time was it two hours and 20 minutes ago?

18. Danielle's watch showed 11:25. Later, it showed 12:30. How much time has passed?

19. Jeff's watch shows 7:55. Earlier, it showed 4:45. How much time has passed?

Student Guide - page 198 (Answers on p. 32)

20. Do an activity for 5 minutes. Write down the time you start and the time you finish. These are some good activities to try: reading, practicing math facts, listening to music, practicing a musical instrument, practicing a sport, running, cleaning your room, and doing chores.

Extension

You can make your own water clock by following these directions.

Materials

- a clear jar with straight sides (A peanut butter jar works well.)
- a large plastic jug with a cap (A milk bottle or soda bottle will do.)
- a hammer and a small nail
- masking tape
- a pair of scissors
- a clock
- food coloring (optional)

Instructions

1. Put a strip of tape from the top to the bottom of your jar, as shown.
2. With an adult's help, use the hammer and nail to make a small hole in the cap of the jug.

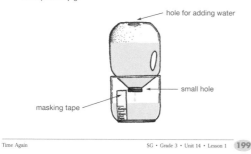

hole for adding water

small hole

masking tape

Student Guide - page 199 *(Answers on p. 32)*

Part 3 Five Minute Activities

After students practice with their clocks, the class can choose an activity to do for five minutes *(Question 20).* Whatever they choose, ask them to read the time on the class clock to the nearest five minutes. After five minutes, ask students to read the class clock again. The class can then choose other activities to do and repeat the same procedure as much as time allows. Possible activities include reading books, playing a game, and practicing the nines multiplication facts with flash cards.

---

3. Put the cap back on the jug.
4. In the bottom of the jug, make a hole large enough so that water can pour through.
5. Turn the jug upside down, and cover the hole in the cap with your finger.
6. Add water to the jug.
7. Place the jug on top of the jar as shown.
8. Let the water drip through the hole in the cap. After 5 minutes, make a mark on the masking tape showing the water level. Keep making marks every 5 minutes for a half hour.
9. Check your clock by emptying the jar and letting the water drip through again. The water should reach each mark at the same time it did before.

In ancient Rome, water clocks were used to time speeches made by lawyers in court. How could you use your clock?

Student Guide - page 200

Name _____ Date _____

Unit 14 Home Practice

PART 1

1. 82 + 69 = _____   2. 472 + 579 = _____
3. 8 × 200 = _____   4. 300 × 5 = _____

5. Find two 2-digit numbers with a sum of 137. _____ and _____

6. The normal temperature for July in Nome, Alaska, is 51°F. In Phoenix, Arizona, it is 92°F.
   A. Usually, how many degrees warmer is it in Phoenix than in Nome for the month of July? _____
   B. What is the normal temperature in San Francisco, California, for July if it is 13 degrees warmer than the normal temperature in Nome? _____
   C. What is the normal temperature in San Antonio, Texas, for July if it is 44 degrees warmer than Nome? _____

PART 2

1. 665 − 456 = _____   2. 604 − 456 = _____
3. 350 + 50 + _____ = 1000   4. 1000 − 350 = _____
5. 250 + 400 + _____ = 1000   6. 1000 − 250 = _____
7. 420 + 100 + _____ = 1000   8. 1000 − 420 = _____

9. Nick's family had to drive 143 miles to visit his grandma for Thanksgiving. Nick asked, "Are we there yet?" His dad said, "We have about 47 miles to go." About how many miles had they driven already?

_____

Discovery Assignment Book - page 216 *(Answers on p. 33)*

Math Facts

DPP Bit A tells students to practice the multiplication facts using the *Triangle Flash Cards: 9s*.

Homework and Practice

- Assign as homework any questions not completed on the *Time Again* Activity Pages in the *Student Guide.*

- DPP Task B provides practice solving problems involving elapsed time.

- Remind students to continue to practice the multiplication facts for the nines using the *Triangle Flash Cards.*

- Part 1 of the Home Practice provides computation practice and may be assigned for homework.

Answers for Part 1 of the Home Practice are in the Answer Key at the end of this lesson and at the end of this unit.

Assessment

- Have students complete the *More Time* Assessment Blackline Master.

- Use the *Observational Assessment Record* to record students' abilities to tell time to the nearest minute and to solve problems involving elapsed time.

Extension

Students can build a water clock as described on the *Time Again* Activity Pages in class or at home.

Literature Connection

- Hutchins, Pat. *Clocks and More Clocks.* Aladdin Paperbacks, Hong Kong, 1994.

This is a story about a man who finds a clock in his attic and becomes confused when he tries to check the time on his attic clock by using clocks in other parts of his house. He reads a clock on another floor of the house and then runs to the attic, only to find that the times are not the same. The illustrations include many clock faces so students can practice telling time as they follow the story.

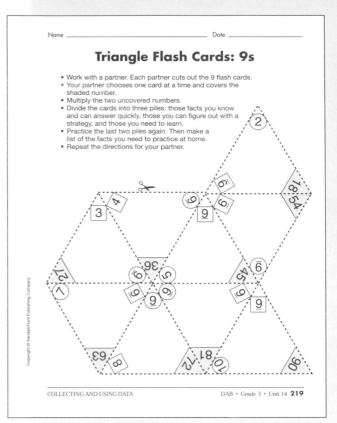

Discovery Assignment Book - page 219

At a Glance

Math Facts and Daily Practice and Problems

DPP Bit A reminds students to practice the multiplication facts using the *Triangle Flash Cards: 9s.* Task B provides problems about elapsed time.

Part 1. Telling Time to the Minute

1. Read the *Time Again* Activity Pages in the *Student Guide* as a class.
2. Review the positions of the hands on a clock and the meaning of each tick mark.
3. Model times to the minute on the demonstration clock and ask students to tell the time.
4. Complete *Questions 1–9* on the *Time Again* Activity Pages in class.

Part 2. Elapsed Time

1. Read and discuss the sample problem on the *Time Again* Activity Pages.
2. Model several problems involving elapsed time.
3. Students practice converting hours to minutes and vice versa.
4. Students complete *Questions 10–20* involving elapsed time on the *Time Again* Activity Pages.

Part 3. Five Minute Activities

1. Students note the time on an analog clock to the nearest five minutes.
2. Students engage in an activity for five minutes.
3. Students note the ending time.

Homework

1. Assign as homework any problems not used in class on the *Time Again* Activity Pages.
2. Assign Part 1 of the Home Practice.
3. Remind students to take home their *Triangle Flash Cards* to study with a family member.

Assessment

1. Students complete the *More Time* Assessment Blackline Master.
2. Use the *Observational Assessment Record* to document students' abilities to tell time to the nearest minute and to solve problems involving elapsed time.

Extension

Have students build a water clock.

Connection

Read and discuss *Clocks and More Clocks* by Pat Hutchins.

Answer Key is on pages 31–33.

Notes:

Clock

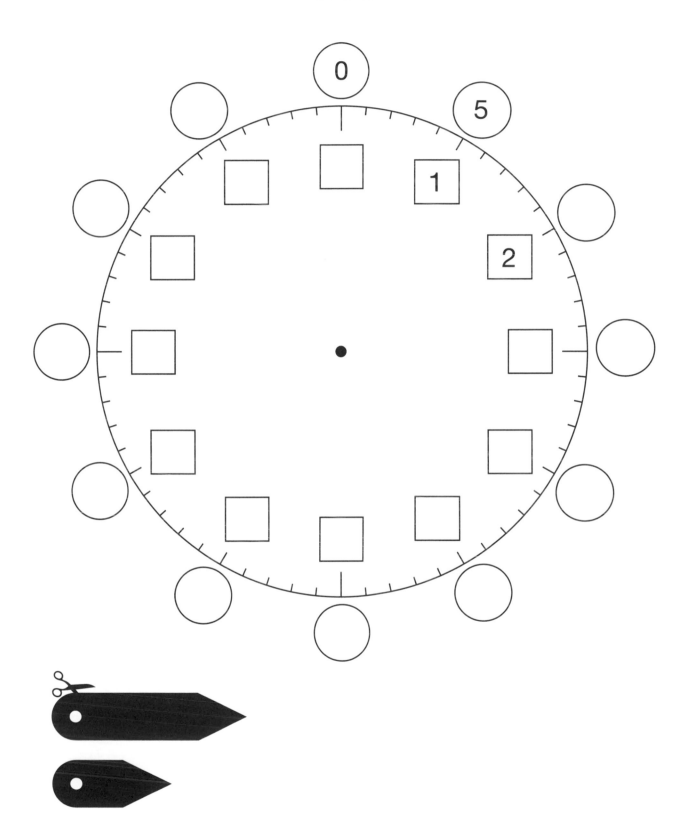

More Time

Write the time shown on each clock. Give each time to the nearest minute.

1. _____   2. _____   3. _____

Answer the following questions in hours and minutes. Then explain how you found your answers.

4. Janet went to see a movie. It started at 7:15. It ended at 9:30. How long was the movie?

5. Brian started playing tennis at 3:35. He played for 55 minutes. What time did Brian stop playing tennis?

6. Keenya spent 125 minutes at the ice rink.
    A. How long is 125 minutes in hours and minutes?
    B. If Keenya left the ice rink at 5:45, what time did she arrive?

Student Guide (p. 196)

1. 10:02
2. 8:22
3. 10:38
4. 7:47
5. 9:07
6. 11:42
7. 4:13
8. 2:32
9. 1:52

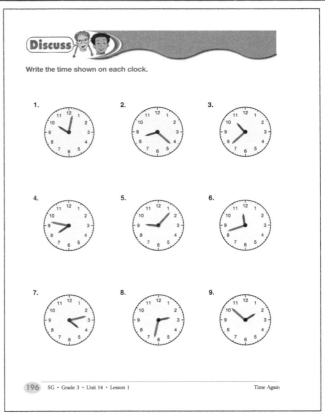

Student Guide - page 196

Student Guide (p. 197)

10. 2 hours and 20 minutes

Student Guide - page 197

11. Seth looked at his watch before and after gymnastics. It showed the following times:

Before   After

How long was Seth's gymnastics practice?

12. Lance went to the store for groceries. He left his apartment at 4:15. He returned home at 4:50. How long did it take Lance to get groceries?

13. Polly went to the park at 10:30 A.M. She returned home at 1:25 P.M. How long was Polly at the park?

14. Rodrigo said it took him 90 minutes to do his homework.
    A. How long is 90 minutes in hours and minutes?
    B. If Rodrigo started his homework at 4:15, what time did he finish?

15. Meghan said it took her 130 minutes to do her homework.
    A. How long is 130 minutes in hours and minutes?
    B. If Meghan started her homework at 3:30, what time did she finish?

16. Sherry's watch shows 3:10. What time was it one hour and 5 minutes ago?

17. Dana's watch shows 5:40. What time was it two hours and 20 minutes ago?

18. Danielle's watch showed 11:25. Later, it showed 12:30. How much time has passed?

19. Jeff's watch shows 7:55. Earlier, it showed 4:45. How much time has passed?

Student Guide - page 198

Student Guide (p. 198)

11. 1 hour and 15 minutes

12. 35 minutes

13. 2 hours and 55 minutes

14. A. 1 hour and 30 minutes
    B. 5:45

15. A. 2 hours and 10 minutes
    B. 5:40

16. 2:05

17. 3:20

18. 1 hour and 5 minutes

19. 3 hours and 10 minutes

---

20. Do an activity for 5 minutes. Write down the time you start and the time you finish. These are some good activities to try: reading, practicing math facts, listening to music, practicing a musical instrument, practicing a sport, running, cleaning your room, and doing chores.

Extension

You can make your own water clock by following these directions.

Materials

- a clear jar with straight sides (A peanut butter jar works well.)
- a large plastic jug with a cap (A milk bottle or soda bottle will do.)
- a hammer and a small nail
- masking tape
- a pair of scissors
- a clock
- food coloring (optional)

Instructions

1. Put a strip of tape from the top to the bottom of your jar, as shown.
2. With an adult's help, use the hammer and nail to make a small hole in the cap of the jug.

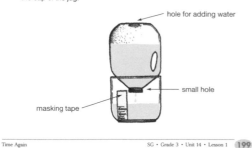

hole for adding water

small hole

masking tape

Student Guide - page 199

Student Guide (p. 199)

20. Answers will vary.

Discovery Assignment Book (p. 216)

Home Practice*

Part 1

 1. 151

 2. 1051

 3. 1600

 4. 1500

 5. Answers will vary. 89 and 48, 99 and 38

 6. **A.** 41 degrees

    B. 64 degrees

    C. 95 degrees

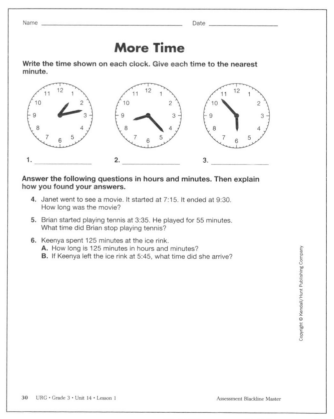

Name _____ Date _____

Unit 14 Home Practice

PART 1

1. 82 + 69 = _____   2. 472 + 579 = _____

3. 8 × 200 = _____   4. 300 × 5 = _____

5. Find two 2-digit numbers with a sum of 137. _____ and _____

6. The normal temperature for July in Nome, Alaska, is 51°F. In Phoenix, Arizona, it is 92°F.

   A. Usually, how many degrees warmer is it in Phoenix than in Nome for the month of July? _____

   B. What is the normal temperature in San Francisco, California, for July if it is 13 degrees warmer than the normal temperature in Nome? _____

   C. What is the normal temperature in San Antonio, Texas, for July if it is 44 degrees warmer than Nome? _____

PART 2

1. 665 − 456 = _____   2. 604 − 456 = _____

3. 350 + 50 + _____ = 1000   4. 1000 − 350 = _____

5. 250 + 400 + _____ = 1000   6. 1000 − 250 = _____

7. 420 + 100 + _____ = 1000   8. 1000 − 420 = _____

9. Nick's family had to drive 143 miles to visit his grandma for Thanksgiving. Nick asked, "Are we there yet?" His dad said, "We have about 47 miles to go." About how many miles had they driven already?

_____

216 DAB • Grade 3 • Unit 14   COLLECTING AND USING DATA

Discovery Assignment Book - page 216

Unit Resource Guide (p. 30)

More Time

 1. 1:13

 2. 8:23

 3. 5:53

 4. 2 hours and 15 minutes

 5. 4:30

 6. **A.** 2 hours and 5 minutes

    B. 3:40

Name _____ Date _____

More Time

Write the time shown on each clock. Give each time to the nearest minute.

1. _____   2. _____   3. _____

Answer the following questions in hours and minutes. Then explain how you found your answers.

4. Janet went to see a movie. It started at 7:15. It ended at 9:30. How long was the movie?

5. Brian started playing tennis at 3:35. He played for 55 minutes. What time did Brian stop playing tennis?

6. Keenya spent 125 minutes at the ice rink.
   A. How long is 125 minutes in hours and minutes?
   B. If Keenya left the ice rink at 5:45, what time did she arrive?

30   URG • Grade 3 • Unit 14 • Lesson 1   Assessment Blackline Master

Unit Resource Guide - page 30

*Answers for all the Home Practice in the *Discovery Assignment Book* are at the end of the unit.

Lesson 2

Time and Time Again

This game is a variation of the card games *Concentration* and *Lotto,* in which players find pairs from memory. In this game, players turn over face-down cards, seeking to match the time on an analog clock to the corresponding digital time.

Key Content

- Telling time to the nearest 5 minutes on analog and digital clocks.

Math Facts

DPP Bit C provides practice with the multiplication facts for the 9s. Task D provides practice with the nines and multiples of ten.

Homework

1. Students take the cards home to play the game with a family member.
2. Assign Part 2 of the Home Practice.

Materials List

Supplies and Copies

Student	Teacher
Supplies for Each Student • scissors	**Supplies**
Copies	**Copies/Transparencies**

All blackline masters including assessment, transparency, and DPP masters are also on the Teacher Resource CD.

Student Books

Time and Time Again (*Student Guide* Page 201)
Time and Time Again Analog Cards (*Discovery Assignment Book* Pages 221–223)
Time and Time Again Digital Cards (*Discovery Assignment Book* Pages 225–227)

Daily Practice and Problems and Home Practice

DPP items C–D (*Unit Resource Guide* Pages 13–14)
Home Practice Part 2 (*Discovery Assignment Book* Page 216)

Note: Classrooms whose pacing differs significantly from the suggested pacing of the units should use the Math Facts Calendar in Section 4 of the *Facts Resource Guide* to ensure students receive the complete math facts program.

C. Bit: Triples (URG p. 13)

1. A. $3 \times 2 =$
   B. $3 \times 3 \times 2 =$
   C. $9 \times 2 =$
2. A. $3 \times 3 =$
   B. $3 \times 3 \times 3 =$
   C. $9 \times 3 =$
3. A. $3 \times 4 =$
   B. $3 \times 3 \times 4 =$
   C. $9 \times 4 =$
4. A. $3 \times 5 =$
   B. $3 \times 3 \times 5 =$
   C. $9 \times 5 =$

D. Task: Multiples of 10 and 100 (URG p. 14)

Use the patterns you found in your multiplication table for multiplying by 10 and 100 to do the following problems.

1. $2 \times 9 =$ 2. $2 \times 90 =$
3. $2 \times 900 =$ 4. $9 \times 7 =$
5. $9 \times 70 =$ 6. $9 \times 700 =$
7. $4 \times 9 =$ 8. $4 \times 90 =$
9. $4 \times 900 =$

Teaching the Game

The *Time and Time Again* Game Page in the *Student Guide* introduces students to the game. Each group of students cuts out the cards on the *Time and Time Again Analog and Digital Cards* Game Pages in the *Discovery Assignment Book.* Players mix one set of the analog and digital card decks and lay out the cards face down. Players turn over pairs, trying to find matching analog and digital times. Play continues until all matches are found. The player with the most pairs is the winner.

TIMS Tip

The analog time cards can be used as flash cards to help students practice telling time.

Journal Prompt

Draw five cards from the mixed deck without looking. Then write a story about someone going somewhere or doing something at each of the times you drew. The times can be in the morning or evening, but your story should say which.

Time and Time Again

Players

This is a game for two or three players.

Materials

- 1 set of *Time and Time Again Analog Cards*
- 1 set of *Time and Time Again Digital Cards*

Rules

1. Mix the two decks together thoroughly.
2. Spread out all the cards face down on a table or desk. (This game is similar to the card games *Concentration* and *Lotto.*)
3. The first player turns over two cards at a time.
4. He or she tries to match an analog clock face with the digital time, as in this picture.

5. If the cards match, the player places them in his or her pile and takes another turn.
6. If the cards do not match, the player's turn is over. He or she should return the two cards to their original face-down position.
7. Players take turns until all the matches are found.
8. The player with the most pairs at the end of the game is the winner.

Time and Time Again   SG • Grade 3 • Unit 14 • Lesson 2   **201**

Student Guide - page 201

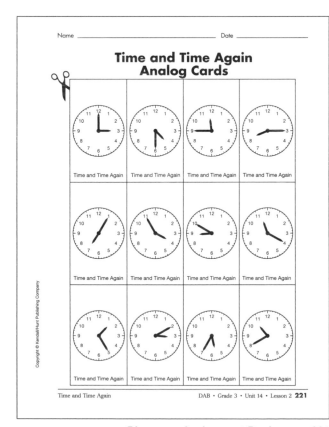

Discovery Assignment Book - page 221

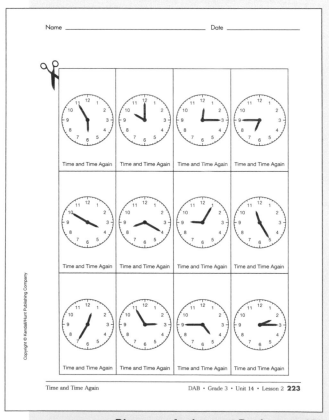

Discovery Assignment Book - page 223

URG • Grade 3 • Unit 14 • Lesson 2   **37**

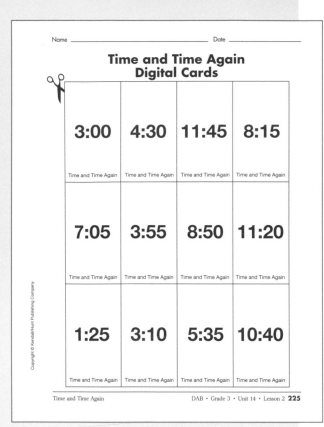

Name _____ Date _____

Time and Time Again
Digital Cards

3:00	**4:30**	**11:45**	**8:15**
Time and Time Again	Time and Time Again	Time and Time Again	Time and Time Again
7:05	**3:55**	**8:50**	**11:20**
Time and Time Again	Time and Time Again	Time and Time Again	Time and Time Again
1:25	**3:10**	**5:35**	**10:40**
Time and Time Again	Time and Time Again	Time and Time Again	Time and Time Again

Time and Time Again   DAB • Grade 3 • Unit 14 • Lesson 2 **225**

Discovery Assignment Book - page 225

Math Facts

DPP Bit C develops strategies for the nines multiplication facts. Task D provides practice with the nines and multiples of ten.

Homework and Practice

• Students can play the game with their families. They should bring home their *Student Guide* and the two decks of cards.

• Part 2 of the Home Practice in the *Discovery Assignment Book* provides computation practice and can be assigned for homework.

Answers for Part 2 of the Home Practice are in the Answer Key at the end of this lesson and at the end of this unit.

Name _____ Date _____

5:55	**10:00**	**12:15**	**6:45**
Time and Time Again	Time and Time Again	Time and Time Again	Time and Time Again
3:50	**8:20**	**9:05**	**11:25**
Time and Time Again	Time and Time Again	Time and Time Again	Time and Time Again
12:35	**2:55**	**4:45**	**2:15**
Time and Time Again	Time and Time Again	Time and Time Again	Time and Time Again

Time and Time Again   DAB • Grade 3 • Unit 14 • Lesson 2 **227**

Discovery Assignment Book - page 227

Name _____ Date _____

Unit 14 Home Practice

PART 1

1. $82 + 69 =$ _____   2. $472 + 579 =$ _____

3. $8 \times 200 =$ _____   4. $300 \times 5 =$ _____

5. Find two 2-digit numbers with a sum of 137. _____ and _____

6. The normal temperature for July in Nome, Alaska, is 51°F. In Phoenix, Arizona, it is 92°F.

   A. Usually, how many degrees warmer is it in Phoenix than in Nome for the month of July? _____

   B. What is the normal temperature in San Francisco, California, for July if it is 13 degrees warmer than the normal temperature in Nome? _____

   C. What is the normal temperature in San Antonio, Texas, for July if it is 44 degrees warmer than Nome? _____

PART 2

1. $665 - 456 =$ _____   2. $604 - 456 =$ _____

3. $350 + 50 +$ _____ $= 1000$ 4. $1000 - 350 =$ _____

5. $250 + 400 +$ _____ $= 1000$ 6. $1000 - 250 =$ _____

7. $420 + 100 +$ _____ $= 1000$ 8. $1000 - 420 =$ _____

9. Nick's family had to drive 143 miles to visit his grandma for Thanksgiving. Nick asked, "Are we there yet?" His dad said, "We have about 47 miles to go." About how many miles had they driven already?

   _____

216 DAB • Grade 3 • Unit 14   COLLECTING AND USING DATA

Discovery Assignment Book - page 216 (Answers on p. 40)

At a Glance

Math Facts and Daily Practice and Problems

DPP Bit C provides practice with the multiplication facts for the 9s. Task D provides practice with the nines and multiples of ten.

Teaching the Game

1. Students cut out the cards on the *Time and Time Again Analog* and *Digital Cards* Game Pages in the *Discovery Assignment Book*.
2. Students read the rules on the *Time and Time Again* Game Page in the *Student Guide*.
3. Students play the game *Time and Time Again*.

Homework

1. Students take the cards home to play the game with a family member.
2. Assign Part 2 of the Home Practice.

Answer Key is on page 40.

Notes:

Name _____ Date _____

Unit 14 Home Practice

PART 1
1. 82 + 69 = _____
2. 472 + 579 = _____
3. 8 × 200 = _____
4. 300 × 5 = _____

5. Find two 2-digit numbers with a sum of 137. _____ and _____

6. The normal temperature for July in Nome, Alaska, is 51°F. In Phoenix, Arizona, it is 92°F.
   A. Usually, how many degrees warmer is it in Phoenix than in Nome for the month of July? _____
   B. What is the normal temperature in San Francisco, California, for July if it is 13 degrees warmer than the normal temperature in Nome? _____
   C. What is the normal temperature in San Antonio, Texas, for July if it is 44 degrees warmer than Nome? _____

PART 2
1. 665 − 456 = _____
2. 604 − 456 = _____
3. 350 + 50 + _____ = 1000
4. 1000 − 350 = _____
5. 250 + 400 + _____ = 1000
6. 1000 − 250 = _____
7. 420 + 100 + _____ = 1000
8. 1000 − 420 = _____

9. Nick's family had to drive 143 miles to visit his grandma for Thanksgiving. Nick asked, "Are we there yet?" His dad said, "We have about 47 miles to go." About how many miles had they driven already?
   _____

Copyright © Kendall/Hunt Publishing Company

216 DAB • Grade 3 • Unit 14   COLLECTING AND USING DATA

Discovery Assignment Book - page 216

Discovery Assignment Book (p. 216)

Home Practice*

Part 2

1. 209
2. 148
3. 600
4. 650
5. 350
6. 750
7. 480
8. 580
9. 96 miles

*Answers for all the Home Practice in the *Discovery Assignment Book* are at the end of the unit.

Lesson 3

Tracking Our Reading

Lesson Overview

Estimated Class Sessions
1-2

This activity is a long-term class project that will continue for two or more weeks. During the first week, the class collects data on students' reading. They record the number of pages and the number of minutes the whole class reads that week. Then they use the data to set a goal for the following week or two. The class continues to collect data to see if they meet their goal. The data collected during the project will be used to introduce the use of familiar percentages, to launch the lab *Make Your Own Survey,* and to provide a context for solving problems involving the addition and subtraction of large numbers. As a side effect of this project, we hope that students will read more.

Key Content

- Telling time to 1 minute.
- Using simple percentages (0%, 25%, 50%, 75%, 100%) as benchmarks.
- Collecting, organizing, and analyzing data.
- Using patterns in data to make predictions and solve problems.

Key Vocabulary

- percent

Math Facts

DPP Bit E provides practice with multiplication facts.

Homework

1. Students will read at home and record their data.
2. Assign Part 3 of the Home Practice.

Materials List

Supplies and Copies

Student	Teacher
Supplies for Each Student	**Supplies** • large sheet of paper or a flip chart for recording class data
Copies • 2 copies of *Eight-column Data Table* per student, optional (*Unit Resource Guide* Page 53)	**Copies/Transparencies** • 1 enlarged (and laminated) copy of *Reading Goal Scale* for the class or 100 cc graduated cylinder and colored water (*Unit Resource Guide* Page 52)

All blackline masters including assessment, transparency, and DPP masters are also on the Teacher Resource CD.

Student Books
Tracking Our Reading (*Student Guide* Page 202)

Daily Practice and Problems and Home Practice
DPP items E–F (*Unit Resource Guide* Pages 14–15)
Home Practice Part 3 (*Discovery Assignment Book* Page 217)

Note: Classrooms whose pacing differs significantly from the suggested pacing of the units should use the Math Facts Calendar in Section 4 of the *Facts Resource Guide* to ensure students receive the complete math facts program.

Daily Practice and Problems

Suggestions for using the DPPs are on page 50.

E. Bit: Fine Nines (URG p. 14)

Do these problems in your head. Write only the answers.

A. $9 \times 1 =$ B. $9 \times 7 =$

C. $8 \times 9 =$ D. $9 \times 2 =$

E. $6 \times 9 =$ F. $9 \times 4 =$

G. $10 \times 9 =$ H. $9 \times 9 =$

I. $9 \times 3 =$ J. $5 \times 9 =$

K. $9 \times 0 =$

F. Task: Six-tenths (URG p. 15)

Draw a rectangle 5 cm long and 4 cm wide. Divide the rectangle into ten equal parts. Color six of the parts.

1. Write a fraction for the shaded area of the rectangle.
2. Write a fraction for the unshaded area.

Before the Activity

You will need a way to chart class progress toward the reading goal. We suggest you hang a poster of the *Reading Goal Scale* Transparency Master on a wall where students can see their progress. You may want to laminate it.

Another option is to prepare a 100 cc graduated cylinder and use its scale to track class progress toward the goal. Place a piece of tape opposite the scale on the cylinder. On this tape, write the total pages of the goal opposite the 100 cc mark, half the goal opposite the 50 cc mark, and so on. Use colored water to show class progress instead of coloring in the scale on the thermometer picture.

Teaching the Activity

Discussion of the activity is divided into three parts:

Part 1: Introducing the project, organizing the data table, and collecting the initial data

Part 2: Analyzing the data, setting a goal, collecting more data, and using a scale to record progress

Part 3: Completing the project and discussing the results

Parts 1 and 2 will be completed during this unit. Part 3, completion of the project, will take place during a later unit. During Part 1, the class decides how they will record the preliminary data. Each day for a week, they record in a data table the number of pages and the number of minutes they read. The end of the first week of data collection will probably coincide with the end of the unit. At that time, the class can begin Part 2 of the project by setting a reading goal for the next week (or next two weeks) based on their collected data. They continue to collect data during the next unit, noting their progress toward their goal as a percentage on a scale. Part 3 allows students to discuss and analyze results at the end of their data collection.

Part 1 Introducing the Project, Organizing the Data Table, and Collecting the Data

To begin the project, explain to students that the class will collect data on their reading for one week and use the data to predict how much the class will read during the following weeks. In the initial lesson, the following issues should be discussed as the class decides how to organize the data.

VARIABLES FOR STUDY

Variable	Possible Values	Comments
time	1 hour, 20 minutes, 16 minutes	The class must decide whether to record the time in minutes or hours and how precise they want the measurements to be. For example, if they measure in hours, they can measure to the nearest quarter hour; if they measure in minutes, to the nearest minute. For practice reading the clock to the nearest 5 minutes, have students record their data to the nearest 5 minutes.
number of books	1 book, 10 books	*Number of books* is an obvious variable to study; however, it is probably more informative to record the number of pages the students read.
number of pages	20 pages, 4 pages	The number of pages students read will provide a context for reviewing addition and subtraction of large numbers later in the unit.

Figure 1: *Table of variables for study*

- **Choosing variables to study.** The table lists variables students can study as part of the project and gives possible values for those variables. Comments on the collection and use of the variables are also included in the table.

Keep in mind that an important goal of this activity is to provide students with practice telling time, calculating the passage of time, and converting between minutes and hours. Therefore, even if your class decides to study number of books or pages, the students should still record beginning and ending times and number of minutes on their data tables.

- **Organizing the data.** Together with the class, design data tables based on the variables the class chooses to study. Individual data tables are needed for each student to record his or her own reading, and a class data table is needed to record the totals for each day. Students can keep individual data tables using the *Eight-column Data Table* or design their own. Post the class data table on a wall or board where it can remain up for several weeks. Figures 2 and 3 show samples of these tables. Note that individual data recorded for a given day (e.g., 3-6-07) will actually be recorded on the class data table on the following day (e.g., 3-7-07), but should be marked correctly (3-6-07).

My Tracking Our Reading Data

Title	Date	Number of Pages	Beginning Time	Ending Time	Number of Minutes	Adult's Initials for Reading at Home	
The Ghostly Galleons	3-6-07	8	10:00 A.M.	10:20 A.M.	20		
Reptiles	3-6-07	2	8:36 P.M.	8:50 P.M.	15	CRK	

Figure 2: *This sample data table could be taken home by students to record home reading.*

Class Tracking Our Reading Data

Date	Number of Pages for Class by Day	Total Pages	Number of Minutes for Class by Day	Total Minutes
3-6-07	420	420	900	900
3-7-07	302	722	790	1690
3-8-07	380	1102	820	2510

Figure 3: *Sample class data table*

TIMS Tip

It might be prudent to ask each student to keep two individual data tables: one to remain at school and the other to travel back and forth between home and school. Students could then transfer their home data to their school data table when they arrive at school each day.

• **Reporting data accurately and fairly.** This unit provides an opportunity for the class to discuss the importance of reporting data accurately and consistently. Children often think of this in terms of "fairness." The class will have to discuss and decide what reading can be recorded. Some examples of things to consider follow. Your class will need to decide if reading counts when . . .

an adult reads to you at home;
a teacher reads to you in school;
it lasts less than 5 minutes;
it is for a social studies report;
it was done last week or last month;
someone reads a magazine or a comic book;
someone reads an article in a newspaper;
someone reads a picture book.

Some students may feel pressure to write down more pages and minutes than are accurate. To reduce some of this pressure, students could report their reading anonymously. (For example, each student copies the new information on his or her data table on a slip of paper and puts it in a "reading mailbox.") Point out to students that they will read different numbers of pages depending on the circumstances. Students reading more difficult books will read fewer pages. On a day when a student has a particularly busy schedule, it is all right for the student to report that he or she did not read any pages at all.

Another way to encourage accurate reporting is to discuss the consequences of using inaccurate data. For example, what if the librarian used the data to predict the number and type of books he or she should order for the library. Scientists, government officials, and many others need to be able to trust that the data they use is accurate. Students will need correct data if they are to make a good prediction for their reading in the weeks to come.

Once students organize the data tables, they are ready to collect the data. They record the data and add it to the class chart each day as part of the Daily Practice and Problems. All students' entries for the day must be added together and the total recorded on the class data table. Then the class can update the running total. They collect data for one week. See Figure 3. As the data accumulates, students can predict the total for the following day.

TIMS Tip

When collecting class data, it may be easier to have students report their data to small groups. Each group can add their data and then report it to the class.

Part 2 Analyzing the Data, Setting a Goal, Collecting More Data, and Using a Scale to Record Progress

At the end of one week, the class analyzes the data. They begin by answering questions similar to the following:

*   *What day did the class read the most (or the least)?*
*   *How many more pages did the class read on Monday than Tuesday?*
*   *How many minutes did we read during the weekend?*
*   *What was the total number of pages read?*

The final objective of this discussion is to set reasonable goals for how many pages and minutes to read in an appropriate period of time. For example, students may decide to read about twice as much in the next two weeks as they read in the past week. Or they may decide that students should try to read one more page per day during the coming week than they did during the previous week. Then they can calculate the total number of pages they will need to read to achieve this goal. Have students round off numbers to make calculations easier. Guide them to pick a realistic goal by using the data.

Tell students they will use percentages to describe how close they are to their goal each day. Ask if any student knows an example of a percentage. Have them discuss what they know. Many will know that 100% of a quantity is all of it and 50% is one-half. In third grade, we only want students to know that a percentage is a fraction. In particular, 25% is one-fourth since it is halfway between 0% and 50%. Moreover, 75% is halfway between 50% and 100%.

Tracking Our Reading

Mr. Wright's class kept track of their reading for one week. Each student counted the number of pages he or she read and reported the number to the class. Altogether the class read 932 pages during the week.

They set a goal of reading 2000 pages during the next two weeks. They kept track of their progress using a percentage "thermometer."

This is how the thermometer looked after they had worked toward their goal for one week. They have one more week to go.

100% — 2000 pages
75% — 1500 pages
50% — 1000 pages
25% — 500 pages
0% — 0 pages

1. The class chose a goal for two weeks based on the 932 pages they read in one week. Did they choose a realistic goal? Why or why not?

2. All of their goal is the same as 100%. To meet their goal, how many pages must they read?

3. Half of their goal is the same as 50% of their goal. How many pages must they read to reach 50% of their goal?

4. One-fourth of their goal is the same as 25%. How many pages must they read to reach 25% of their goal?

5. Three-fourths of their goal is the same as 75%. How many pages must they read to reach 75% of their goal?

6. Do you think Mr. Wright's students will reach their goal by the end of the two weeks? Why or why not?

You and your classmates will choose a reading goal and show your progress using percentages.

202   SG • Grade 3 • Unit 14 • Lesson 3   Tracking Our Reading

Student Guide - page 202 *(Answers on p. 54)*

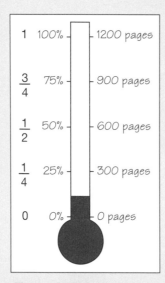

Figure 4: *The scale for a class whose progress is 135 pages and whose goal is 1200 pages*

The *Tracking Our Reading* Activity Page in the *Student Guide* provides discussion questions that will help the class choose an appropriate goal and introduce students to the use of simple percentages to record progress towards their goal. *Question 1* asks if students in Mr. Wright's class chose a realistic goal. Since his students read 932 pages in one week, a goal of 2000 pages is realistic for a two week period since 2000 is about two times 932.

Questions 2–5 ask students how many pages the class needs to read to meet 100, 50, 25, and 75 percent of their goal. Students can read these numbers directly from the percentage thermometer pictured on the page. As you discuss each question, ask students to explain how to find the number of pages corresponding to each percentage of the goal. For example, ask why 1000 is 50% of 2000. Students should see that 50% of 2000 is the same as one-half of 2000, or 1000.

Question 6 asks if Mr. Wright's class will reach the goal. Since the thermometer shows that the class has read more than 1000 pages at the end of the first week, the students will probably meet or pass their goal by the end of two weeks.

After students finish discussing the questions on the *Tracking Our Reading* Activity Page, they choose a goal based on the data collected in the first part of the activity. Once the class chooses a goal, show them the scale you made from the *Reading Goal Scale* Transparency Master. This will be used to chart their progress. The scale, which is on a thermometer, is divided into fourths that are labeled 0, 25, 50, 75, and 100 percent on the left-hand side. The right-hand side is left blank. Ask students which fractions represent 25%, 50%, and 75% on the scale as shown in Figure 4. Have individual students label 0, $\frac{1}{4}$, $\frac{1}{2}$, $\frac{3}{4}$, and 1 on the scale. Use the language of fractions to introduce the language of percents as the class works together to write the number of pages on the right-hand side of the scale. For example, if a class chose 1200 pages as their goal, they would number the scale as shown in Figure 4. Begin by telling students that 100 percent represents one whole; then, continue the discussion using questions similar to those presented here. The questions and the discussion use 1200 pages as an example goal. A goal expressed as number of minutes is equally valid.

• *What is our goal? What number should we write opposite 100 percent?* (Since 1200 pages is the goal, write 1200 there.)

• *If 100 percent represents the whole, what would 50 percent represent?* (one-half)

• *What is 50 percent of our goal?* (600 pages)

- *What should we write opposite 50 percent?* (600 pages)
- *If 100 percent is one whole and 50 percent is the same as one-half, what percent represents one-fourth?* (25 percent is the same as one-fourth.)
- *What is one-fourth of 1200 pages?* (Since one-fourth is halfway between 0 and $\frac{1}{2}$ and 300 is halfway between 0 and 600, 300 is one-fourth of 1200.)
- *What should we write opposite 25 percent?* (300 pages)
- *What should we write opposite 75 percent?* (75 percent is halfway between 50 percent and 100 percent. Since 900 pages is halfway between 600 and 1200 pages, 900 pages is 75% of 1200 pages.)

Students may also relate the percents to money and compare 50 percent to 50 cents, 25 percent to one quarter, and 75 cents to three quarters. At each step, encourage students to justify their responses.

During the time allowed by the class to reach their goal, data collection will continue as in the first week. As the class data table is updated, color in the thermometer to represent the daily progress toward the goal. (Or, if you are using the graduated cylinder, add colored water in the same fashion.) Help the class estimate the amount to color. If the class reads 135 pages the first day and the goal is 1200 pages, color in a little less than half of the distance between 0 and 25 percent since 135 is a little less than halfway between 0 and 300.

Part 3 Completing the Project and Discussing the Results

This part of the project will take place after the data collection, an amount of time your students will determine—probably one or two weeks. Therefore this activity will conclude during a succeeding unit. When all the data is collected, take time to discuss the results. Use these discussion prompts or come up with some of your own.

- *Did the class meet or exceed the goal? Why or why not?*
- *On which days (or days of the week) did the class read the most? The least?*
- *Did the class read more or less than was expected?*
- *Could you have made a better prediction? How?*
- *If the class were to set a new goal, what would it be?*

Journal Prompt

Think of the experiments you have done this year. Choose one to write about. Why was it important to record accurate data for that experiment? What could happen in that experiment if the data were not accurate?

Name _____ Date _____

PART 3

1. How many hops, starting at 0, will it take a +9 mathhopper to pass 80? _____ What number will it land on? _____

2. Measure the perimeter of the rectangle below to the nearest half of a centimeter. _____

3. How many rectangles are in the figure below? _____

PART 4

1. How many 30-minute periods are there from 3:00 P.M. until 10:00 P.M.? _____

2. Nine hundred fifty-two is . . .

   A. 100 more than _____   B. 50 more than _____

   C. 50 less than _____   D. about twice _____

3. Find one way that you can divide five $100 bills, eight $50 bills, and five $20 bills into two equal shares.

   _____

   _____

COLLECTING AND USING DATA   DAB • Grade 3 • Unit 14 **217**

***Discovery Assignment Book - page 217** (Answers on p. 54)*

- *Predict the amount the class would read in five weeks or 10 weeks.*
- *Looking at the data now, which variable do you think is the better variable to study, the number of minutes or the number of pages?*

Math Facts

DPP Bit E provides practice with the multiplication facts for the nines.

Homework and Practice

- Students will read at home and record the appropriate data in their data tables. If students decide it will help keep things fair, adults can initial next to home reading times.
- DPP Task F requires students to find a fractional part of a geometric figure.
- Assign Part 3 of the Home Practice for homework.

Answers for Part 3 of the Home Practice are in the Answer Key at the end of this lesson and at the end of this unit.

Extension

Individual students can set goals for themselves using their own data tables. These students can record their progress toward their personal goals using a smaller version of the scale.

Math Facts and Daily Practice and Problems

DPP Bit E provides practice with multiplication facts. Task F is a problem about representing fractions.

Part 1. Introducing the Project, Organizing the Data Table, and Collecting the Data

1. Explain that the class will collect data on their reading for one week.
2. Students choose variables to study: amount of time, number of books, or number of pages.
3. Students design data tables based on the variables they chose to study.
4. Discuss the importance of reporting data accurately.
5. To collect reliable data, students define the variables carefully.
6. Students keep individual data tables of their reading and report to the class each day.
7. Students' entries are added together each day and recorded on the class data table.
8. Students predict the total for the following day.

Part 2. Analyzing the Data, Setting a Goal, Collecting More Data, and Using a Scale to Record Progress

1. As a class, students analyze the data collected during the week.
2. Students set goals about how many pages and minutes to read in an appropriate time.
3. Students complete the *Tracking Our Reading* Activity Page in the *Student Guide.*
4. Students discuss the benchmark percentages: 25%, 50%, 75%, and 100%.
5. Introduce the poster of the *Reading Goal Scale* Transparency Master or the graduated cylinder that will be used to chart students' progress.
6. Discuss the fraction that each percentage represents and write $0, \frac{1}{4}, \frac{1}{2}, \frac{3}{4}$, and 1 next to the appropriate percentages.
7. Students determine the number that represents 25%, 50%, and 75% of the goal.
8. Data collection continues over a period of time and students update the class data table and scale each day.

Part 3. Completing the Project and Discussing the Results

When all the data is collected, discuss the results as a class.

Homework

1. Students will read at home and record their data.
2. Assign Part 3 of the Home Practice.

Extension

After students set personal reading goals, they then track and record their progress.

Answer Key is on page 54.

Notes:

Reading Goal Scale

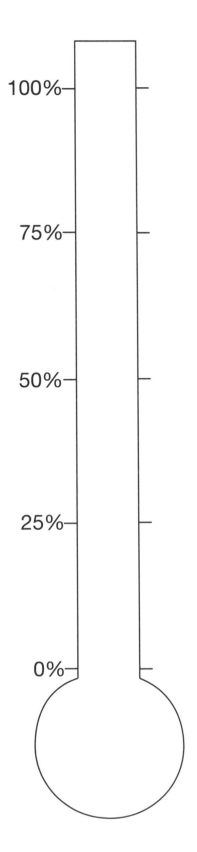

Transparency Master

Name

Date

Eight-column Data Table, Blackline Master

Tracking Our Reading

Mr. Wright's class kept track of their reading for one week. Each student counted the number of pages he or she read and reported the number to the class. Altogether the class read 932 pages during the week.

They set a goal of reading 2000 pages during the next two weeks. They kept track of their progress using a percentage "thermometer."

This is how the thermometer looked after they had worked toward their goal for one week. They have one more week to go.

1. The class chose a goal for two weeks based on the 932 pages they read in one week. Did they choose a realistic goal? Why or why not?

2. All of their goal is the same as 100%. To meet their goal, how many pages must they read?

3. Half of their goal is the same as 50% of their goal. How many pages must they read to reach 50% of their goal?

4. One-fourth of their goal is the same as 25%. How many pages must they read to reach 25% of their goal?

5. Three-fourths of their goal is the same as 75%. How many pages must they read to reach 75% of their goal?

6. Do you think Mr. Wright's students will reach their goal by the end of the two weeks? Why or why not?

You and your classmates will choose a reading goal and show your progress using percentages.

202 SG • Grade 3 • Unit 14 • Lesson 3   Tracking Our Reading

Student Guide - page 202

Student Guide (p. 202)

1. Yes; in one week they read close to 1000 pages. In two weeks they could very well read 2000 pages.

2. 2000 pages

3. 1000 pages

4. 500 pages

5. 1500 pages

6. Yes; the thermometer shows they have passed the halfway mark, (1000 pages or 50% of the pages) in one week. They have one more week to read about 1000 more.

Name _____ Date _____

PART 3

1. How many hops, starting at 0, will it take a +9 mathhopper to pass 80? _____ What number will it land on? _____

2. Measure the perimeter of the rectangle below to the nearest half of a centimeter. _____

3. How many rectangles are in the figure below? _____

PART 4

1. How many 30-minute periods are there from 3:00 P.M. until 10:00 P.M.?
_____

2. Nine hundred fifty-two is . . .
   A. 100 more than _____   B. 50 more than _____
   C. 50 less than _____   D. about twice _____

3. Find one way that you can divide five $100 bills, eight $50 bills, and five $20 bills into two equal shares.
_____
_____

COLLECTING AND USING DATA   DAB • Grade 3 • Unit 14 **217**

Discovery Assignment Book - page 217

Discovery Assignment Book (p. 217)

Home Practice*

Part 3

1. 9 hops; 81

2. 18 cm (7 cm + 2 cm + 7 cm + 2 cm)

3. 9

*Answers for all the Home Practice in the *Discovery Assignment Book* are at the end of the unit.

Lesson 4

Make Your Own Survey

Lesson Overview

Estimated Class Sessions

2-3

Students work in groups to gather survey data about other classmates. This lab provides students with the experience to independently choose a variable to investigate; collect, organize, and graph the data, and then present their findings to the class. The importance of reporting data accurately and honestly is discussed.

Key Content

- Identifying and using variables in a survey.
- Collecting, organizing, graphing, and analyzing data.
- Dealing with precision and accuracy.

Key Vocabulary

- survey

Math Facts

DPP Bit G is the Multiplication Quiz: 9s. Task J reviews square numbers.

Homework

1. Students bring examples of survey data from newspapers or magazines.
2. Assign Part 4 of the Home Practice.

Assessment

1. Assign scores to students' surveys and record comments on their performance using the *TIMS Laboratory Method Checklist* and the *TIMS Multidimensional Rubric*.
2. Use DPP Bit G to assess students' fluency with the multiplication facts for the nines.

Curriculum Sequence

Before This Unit

TIMS Laboratory Method

Students completed laboratory investigations in Grade 3 Unit 1 Lesson 3 *Kind of Bean,* Unit 5 Lesson 3 *The Better "Picker Upper,"* Unit 9 Lesson 1 *Measuring Mass,* and Unit 10 Lesson 1 *Stencilrama.*

After This Unit

TIMS Laboratory Method

Students will use the TIMS Laboratory Method again in Unit 15 Lesson 4 *Length vs. Number,* Unit 16 Lesson 2 *Fill 'er Up,* and Unit 20 Lesson 2 *Tower Power.*

Materials List

Supplies and Copies

Student	Teacher
Supplies for Each Student Group • class names list	**Supplies**
Copies • 1–2 copies of *Centimeter Graph Paper* per student (*Unit Resource Guide* Page 65) • 1 *Three-column, Four-column, Five-column,* or *Eight-column Data Table* per student as selected (*Unit Resource Guide* Pages 53 & 66–68) • 1 *TIMS Laboratory Method Checklist* per student pair for assessment, optional (*Unit Resource Guide* Page 64)	**Copies/Transparencies** • 1 transparency of *Three-column Data Table,* optional (*Unit Resource Guide* Page 66) • 1 transparency of *Centimeter Graph Paper,* optional (*Unit Resource Guide* Page 65)

All blackline masters including assessment, transparency, and DPP masters are also on the Teacher Resource CD.

Student Books

Make Your Own Survey (*Student Guide* Pages 203–208)

Daily Practice and Problems and Home Practice

DPP items G–J (*Unit Resource Guide* Pages 15–16)
Home Practice Part 4 (*Discovery Assignment Book* Page 217)

Note: Classrooms whose pacing differs significantly from the suggested pacing of the units should use the Math Facts Calendar in Section 4 of the *Facts Resource Guide* to ensure students receive the complete math facts program.

Assessment Tools

TIMS Multidimensional Rubric (*Teacher Implementation Guide,* Assessment section)

Daily Practice and Problems

Suggestions for using the DPPs are on page 62.

G. Bit: Multiplication Quiz: 9s (URG p. 15)

A. $3 \times 9 =$ 　　　B. $9 \times 7 =$

C. $10 \times 9 =$ 　　D. $0 \times 9 =$

E. $5 \times 9 =$ 　　　F. $9 \times 8 =$

G. $6 \times 9 =$ 　　　H. $4 \times 9 =$

I. $9 \times 9 =$ 　　　J. $9 \times 2 =$

K. $9 \times 1 =$

I. Bit: Tracking Our Reading 1
(URG p. 16)

Record your reading data the way your class decided.

H. Task: Some Percents (URG p. 16)

What is 50% of

A. 20? 　　　　B. 40?

C. 17? 　　　　D. 1000?

What is 25% of

E. 20? 　　　　F. 40?

G. 17? 　　　　H. 1000?

J. Task: Square Numbers
(URG p. 16)

1. What square number is shown by all the small squares below?

2. What other square numbers do you see?
3. Bob thinks 8 is a square number. Show him why it is not.

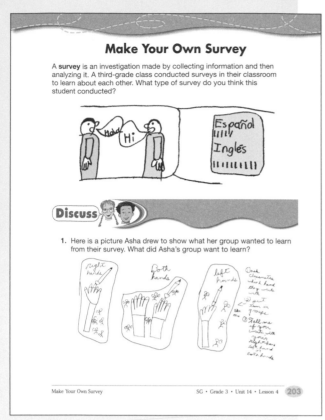

Student Guide - page 203 *(Answers on p. 69)*

Often groups have difficulty agreeing on the variable to choose for their surveys. Forming student groups based on their interests can minimize the time taken for choosing variables.

Discuss the information on the *Make Your Own Survey* Lab Pages in the *Student Guide*. The first two pages define the term **survey** and give examples of student drawings depicting typical surveys.

After students discuss the surveys illustrated on the *Make Your Own Survey* Lab Pages, the class can generate a list of variables they might want to study in a survey. To make the project manageable for students, limit their choice of variables to categorical variables that describe a single characteristic of the students in the room. In other words, they should choose a simple variable with values that are not numbers. For example, hair color and favorite sport are more appropriate choices than height. If students were to select the variable height, they would have to choose appropriate numerical scales for both axes. This could easily become confusing for students without direct instruction from the teacher. Selecting a categorical variable will allow students to work more independently.

The following chart lists variables student groups have chosen to study.

Possible Survey Variables	Values
favorite color	red, blue, green, yellow
favorite type of book	mystery, realistic fiction, science fiction, sports
type of transportation to school	walking, car, bus, bike
languages spoken	English, Spanish, Russian, Urdu, French
favorite subject	math, reading, science, social studies
favorite sport	baseball, basketball, football, soccer

Student Guide - page 204 *(Answers on p. 69)*

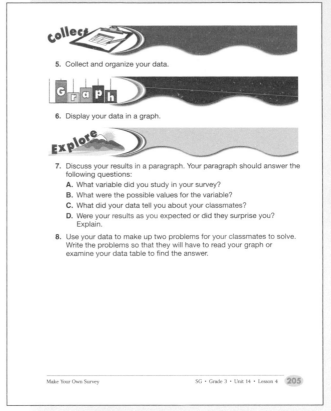

Student Guide - page 205 *(Answers on p. 69)*

At this point, students continue with the lab by reading *Questions 3–8* in the Explore section of the *Make Your Own Survey* Lab Pages. These questions outline the steps students will take in this lab.

If you believe your students need more guidance, model how to conduct the survey. For an example you could collect data on the variable Types of Books since students are currently collecting numerical data about their reading as part of the *Tracking Our Reading* activity. Displaying a transparency of *Three-column Data Table* on the overhead, write a set of values in the rows of the data table such as modern fiction, historical fiction, science fiction, fantasy, and nonfiction. Remind students that they will tally the responses as they conduct the survey and report the totals when they finish. (Therefore, the columns might be labeled Type of Book, Tallies, and Total Number of Students as shown in Figure 5.)

Type of Book	Tallies	Total Number of Students
modern fiction	⁜⁜⁜⁜	5
historical fiction	‖	2
science fiction	⁜⁜⁜⁜ ⁜⁜⁜⁜ ‖	12
fantasy	⁜⁜⁜⁜ ‖	6
nonfiction	‖‖	3

Figure 5: *A sample data table of survey data*

Model making the graph on a transparency of *Centimeter Graph Paper.* Have the class help you choose the title, the labels for the axes, and an appropriate scale for the vertical axis. See Figure 6. Analyze the graph in a class discussion, using questions similar to **Questions 7A–7D** of the Explore section of the *Make Your Own Survey* Lab Pages.

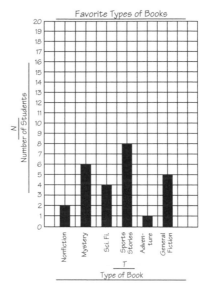

Figure 6: *A sample graph of survey data*

When students are ready to work on the lab independently, they can proceed with minimal instruction using their books as a guide. Discuss the importance of students' answering each group's questions honestly and accurately. To organize their data, groups can choose from a selection of data tables or create their own. Provide each group with a class list so they will know when they have surveyed every student in the room.

The next section of the *Make Your Own Survey* Lab Pages is Survey Questions. You can use these questions as part of the introduction before students begin the lab or as follow-up questions after the lab is completed. **Question 9** in the Survey Questions section provides a data table that a group of students used to survey hair color. Their list of hair colors includes both blond and golden. Students can discuss whether both of these values should be included in the table.

Journal Prompt

How did you help your group with your survey? What did you do as a member of your group?

Survey Questions

9. Julia's group chose the variable *hair color* for their survey. Here is their data table. Do you think they chose good values to write in the data table? Why or why not?

Hair Color

Hair Color	N
dark brown	卌 ||||
light brown	|||
blonde	卌
black	||
golden	卌

Student Guide - page 206 *(Answers on p. 70)*

Questions 10–15 refer to a graph depicting data about whether students in a class stayed at school for lunch or went home. The student who conducted the survey used a scale numbered by 5s on the vertical axis which makes it hard to read the graph. For *Question 13,* students must decide if the scale is appropriate and choose another scale if they think it is inappropriate. If the graph were scaled by ones or twos, it would be easier to read. *Question 14* provides students with another opportunity to discuss the importance of reporting accurate data. Accurate reporting is an important issue in this unit since students answer each other's survey questions and since the class collects data for the *Tracking Our Reading* activity. *Question 15* asks students to make a prediction about the lunch habits of 100 students based on the data in a graph. Since there were about 25 students represented in all the data given, students can multiply both numbers (those who stay for lunch and those who go home) by 4 to make a sound prediction.

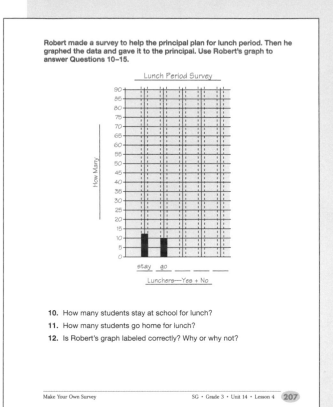

Robert made a survey to help the principal plan for lunch period. Then he graphed the data and gave it to the principal. Use Robert's graph to answer Questions 10–15.

10. How many students stay at school for lunch?
11. How many students go home for lunch?
12. Is Robert's graph labeled correctly? Why or why not?

Make Your Own Survey   SG • Grade 3 • Unit 14 • Lesson 4   207

Student Guide - page 207 *(Answers on p. 70)*

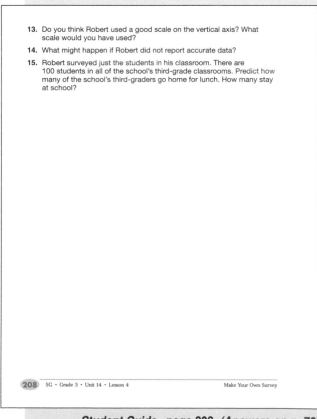

13. Do you think Robert used a good scale on the vertical axis? What scale would you have used?
14. What might happen if Robert did not report accurate data?
15. Robert surveyed just the students in his classroom. There are 100 students in all of the school's third-grade classrooms. Predict how many of the school's third-graders go home for lunch. How many stay at school?

208   SG • Grade 3 • Unit 14 • Lesson 4   Make Your Own Survey

Student Guide - page 208 *(Answers on p. 70)*

Name _____ Date _____

PART 3

1. How many hops, starting at 0, will it take a +9 mathhopper to pass 80? _____ What number will it land on? _____

2. Measure the perimeter of the rectangle below to the nearest half of a centimeter. _____

3. How many rectangles are in the figure below? _____

PART 4

1. How many 30-minute periods are there from 3:00 P.M. until 10:00 P.M.?

   _____

2. Nine hundred fifty-two is . . .

   A. 100 more than _____   B. 50 more than _____

   C. 50 less than _____   D. about twice _____

3. Find one way that you can divide five $100 bills, eight $50 bills, and five $20 bills into two equal shares.

   _____

   _____

Discovery Assignment Book - page 217 *(Answers on p. 71)*

Math Facts

DPP Task J reviews square numbers.

Homework and Practice

- Ask students to bring in examples of survey data from newspapers or magazines. Have the class discuss the variables and critique the display of the data.

- DPP Task H provides practice with 50% and 25%. Bit I reminds the class to collect reading data.

- Assign Part 4 of the Home Practice.

Answers for Part 4 of the Home Practice are in the Answer Key at the end of this lesson and at the end of this unit.

Assessment

- This activity can serve as an assessment of students' abilities to work in groups and to collect, organize, graph, and analyze data. Assign scores to students' surveys and record comments on their performance using the *TIMS Laboratory Method Checklist* Assessment Blackline Master. The *TIMS Multidimensional Rubric* can guide you in assigning scores to their written work. Include the surveys in students' portfolios.

- Students complete Multiplication Quiz: 9s in DPP Bit G.

Extension

Students can conduct a similar experiment at home, surveying family and friends, or they can conduct surveys in other classrooms.

At a Glance

Math Facts and Daily Practice and Problems

DPP Bit G is the Multiplication Quiz: 9s. Task H provides practice with percents. Bit I is a collection of reading data. Task J reviews square numbers.

Teaching the Lab

1. Students read and discuss the first two pages of the *Make Your Own Survey* Lab Pages in the *Student Guide*.
2. Students generate a list of possible variables to study, limiting their choice to categorical variables that describe a single characteristic of the students in the room.
3. Students read *Questions 3–8* on the *Make Your Own Survey* Lab Pages.
4. If students need guidance, model how to conduct the survey, tally the data, and graph the results.
5. To prepare for collecting data, student groups choose from a selection of data tables or create their own.
6. Use Survey Questions on the *Make Your Own Survey* Lab Pages as part of the introduction before students begin the lab or as follow-up questions after the lab.
7. Student groups survey their classmates and record and display their data using the TIMS Laboratory Method.

Homework

1. Students bring examples of survey data from newspapers or magazines.
2. Assign Part 4 of the Home Practice.

Assessment

1. Assign scores to students' surveys and record comments on their performance using the *TIMS Laboratory Method Checklist* and the *TIMS Multidimensional Rubric*.
2. Use DPP Bit G to assess students' fluency with the multiplication facts for the nines.

Extension

Have students conduct a similar experiment at home or in other classrooms.

Answer Key is on pages 69–71.

Notes:

Name _____ Date _____

TIMS Laboratory Method Checklist

Student _____ Date _____

Other Group Members _____

Need Help with:	Score	Comments
Drawing a picture		
Defining variables to investigate		
Defining controlled variables		
Labeling data table		
Collecting and organizing data		
Choosing type of graph		
Labeling axes on graph		
Numbering axes on graph		
Plotting data on graph		
Interpreting results		

Student _____ Date _____

Other Group Members _____

Need Help with:	Score	Comments
Drawing a picture		
Defining variables to investigate		
Defining controlled variables		
Labeling data table		
Collecting and organizing data		
Choosing type of graph		
Labeling axes on graph		
Numbering axes on graph		
Plotting data on graph		
Interpreting results		

Assessment Blackline Master

Name _____ Date _____

_____

Three-column Data Table, Blackline Master

Name _____ Date _____

_____

Four-column Data Table, Blackline Master

Name _____ Date _____

_____

Five-column Data Table, Blackline Master

Student Guide (pp. 203–205)

Make Your Own Survey*

1. Asha's group wanted to learn who is right-handed, who is left-handed, and who uses both hands.

2. **A.** Type of Toothpaste used

   B. Glow, Bright, Fresh, and Clean

3.–8. See the chart in the Lesson Guide for possible survey variables.

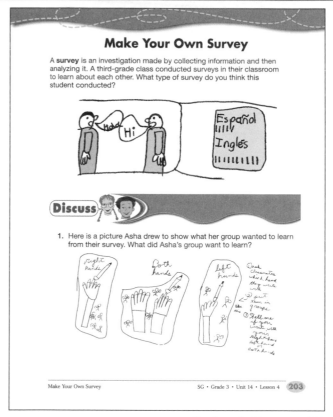

Student Guide - page 203

Student Guide - page 204

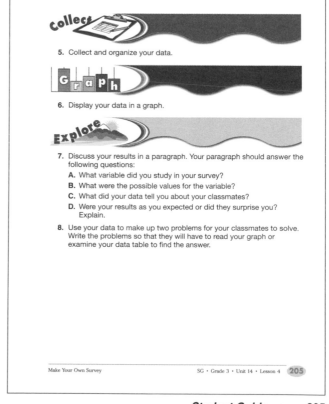

Student Guide - page 205

*Answers and/or discussion are included in the Lesson Guide.

Survey Questions

9. Julia's group chose the variable *hair color* for their survey. Here is their data table. Do you think they chose good values to write in the data table? Why or why not?

Hair Color

Hair Color	N
dark brown	⊬⊬ ‖‖
light brown	‖‖
blonde	⊬⊬
black	‖
golden	⊬⊬

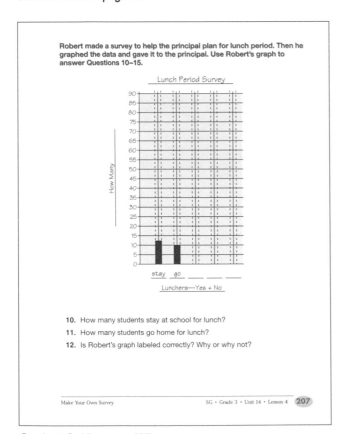

Student Guide - page 206

Student Guide (pp. 206–208)

9. Julia's group lists both blond and golden. It may be difficult to distinguish between the two. One value, such as blond, may have been enough.

10. 12–13 stay

11. 10 go home

12. A better label for the vertical axis may be "Number of Students." "How many" may be unclear. How many what? A better label for the horizontal axis is "Where is lunch eaten?" "Lunchers—Yes + No" sounds as if Robert asked whether each student eats lunch. The two values are not yes and no but rather stay or go.

13. If the graph were scaled by ones or twos, it would be easier to read.

14. If Robert did not report accurate data, the lunchroom may not have enough lunches for those who stay at school.

15. Predictions will vary. Between 54 and 58 stay and between 46 and 42 go home.

Robert made a survey to help the principal plan for lunch period. Then he graphed the data and gave it to the principal. Use Robert's graph to answer Questions 10–15.

10. How many students stay at school for lunch?

11. How many students go home for lunch?

12. Is Robert's graph labeled correctly? Why or why not?

Student Guide - page 207

13. Do you think Robert used a good scale on the vertical axis? What scale would you have used?

14. What might happen if Robert did not report accurate data?

15. Robert surveyed just the students in his classroom. There are 100 students in all of the school's third-grade classrooms. Predict how many of the school's third-graders go home for lunch. How many stay at school?

Student Guide - page 208

Discovery Assignment Book (p. 217)

Home Practice*

Part 4

1. 14

2. **A.** 852

   B. 902

   C. 1002

   D. Answers will vary. 450–500

3. Answers will vary. One possible way to divide is: One person gets the five $100 bills. The other person gets the $50 bills and the $20 bills.

Name _____ Date _____

PART 3

1. How many hops, starting at 0, will it take a +9 mathhopper to pass 80? _____ What number will it land on? _____

2. Measure the perimeter of the rectangle below to the nearest half of a centimeter. _____

3. How many rectangles are in the figure below? _____

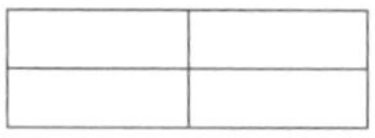

PART 4

1. How many 30-minute periods are there from 3:00 P.M. until 10:00 P.M.? _____

2. Nine hundred fifty-two is . . .

   A. 100 more than _____   **B.** 50 more than _____

   C. 50 less than _____   **D.** about twice _____

3. Find one way that you can divide five $100 bills, eight $50 bills, and five $20 bills into two equal shares.

   _____

   _____

COLLECTING AND USING DATA   DAB • Grade 3 • Unit 14 **217**

Discovery Assignment Book - page 217

---

*Answers for all the Home Practice in the *Discovery Assignment Book* are at the end of the unit.

Lesson 5

Reviewing Addition and Subtraction

Lesson Overview

Estimated Class Sessions

2-3

Students review adding and subtracting large numbers using base-ten pieces and pencil and paper. First, the class discusses examples in the *Student Guide*. Then using the data from *Tracking Our Reading* as a context, students solve problems involving addition and subtraction.

Key Content

- Representing addition and subtraction with base-ten pieces.
- Adding and subtracting multidigit numbers using pencil and paper.
- Solving problems involving addition and subtraction.

Homework

Assign the Homework section on the *Reviewing Addition and Subtraction* Activity Pages.

Assessment

1. Students complete the *Addition and Subtraction* Assessment Blackline Master.
2. Use the *Observational Assessment Record* to note students' abilities to represent multidigit addition and subtraction problems using base-ten pieces.
3. Transfer appropriate documentation from the Unit 14 *Observational Assessment Record* to the students' *Individual Assessment Record Sheets*.

Before This Unit

Students used base-ten pieces to represent multidigit addition in Unit 4 and both addition and subtraction in Unit 6. Working with the pieces, they developed algorithms for solving addition and subtraction problems using pencil and paper.

Materials List

Supplies and Copies

Student	Teacher
Supplies for Each Student • set of base-ten pieces (2 packs, 14 flats, 30 skinnies, and 50 bits)	**Supplies** • set of base-ten pieces • magnetic base-ten pieces and a magnetic board or overhead base-ten pieces, optional
Copies • 1 copy of *Addition and Subtraction* per student (*Unit Resource Guide* Pages 80–81)	**Copies/Transparencies**

All blackline masters including assessment, transparency, and DPP masters are also on the Teacher Resource CD.

Student Books
Reviewing Addition and Subtraction (*Student Guide* Pages 209–215)

Daily Practice and Problems and Home Practice
DPP items K–N (*Unit Resource Guide* Pages 17–18)

Note: Classrooms whose pacing differs significantly from the suggested pacing of the units should use the Math Facts Calendar in Section 4 of the *Facts Resource Guide* to ensure students receive the complete math facts program.

Assessment Tools
Observational Assessment Record (*Unit Resource Guide* Pages 9–10)
Individual Assessment Record Sheet (*Teacher Implementation Guide,* Assessment section)

Suggestions for using the DPPs are on page 78.

K. Bit: Tracking Our Reading 2
(URG p. 17)

Record your reading data the way your class decided.

M. Bit: Tracking Our Reading 3
(URG p. 17)

Record your reading data the way your class decided.

L. Task: Counting by Thirds
(URG p. 17)

Skip counting by thirds backwards from 10.

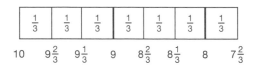

N. Challenge: Adding and Subtracting

(URG p. 18)

Solve the following problems on a sheet of paper. Use base-ten pieces or base-ten shorthand if it helps. Estimate to be sure your answers are reasonable.

1. 137
   + 446

2. 439
   − 176

3. 2348
   + 4769

4. 504
   − 426

5. Explain your estimation strategy for Question 3.

6. Explain how to do Question 4 using mental math.

The *Reviewing Addition and Subtraction* Activity Pages in the *Student Guide* provide examples of students solving multidigit addition and subtraction problems using base-ten pieces, shorthand, and pencil and paper. Begin the activity by discussing these examples as a class and then use manipulatives to work through the examples.

The first example displays a partial solution to a multidigit addition problem using base-ten pieces. *Question 1* encourages students to think through the process and to complete the problem correctly. As students work through the problem, ask them what numbers are represented with the base-ten pieces. Note that the correct answer is 1140 minutes not 114. Ethan forgot to put a 0 in the ones place on his recording sheet. *Question 2* asks students to solve the problem using pencil and paper. Encourage students to explain their thinking and any marks they used to indicate regroupings. Note that a quick estimate would tell Ethan to go back and check his work.

The second example displays a solution to another multidigit addition problem using base-ten shorthand. Have students work through the problem using their own base-ten pieces or ask them to explain the procedure in words.

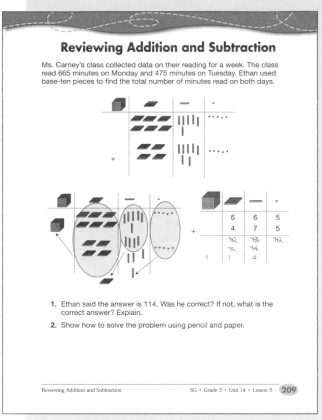

Student Guide - page 209 (Answers on p. 82)

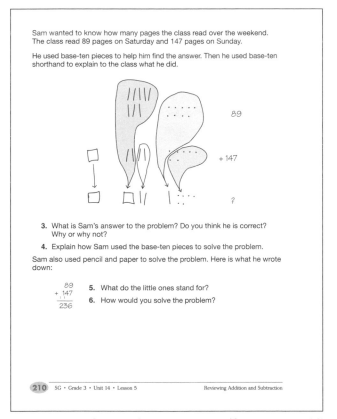

Student Guide - page 210 (Answers on p. 82)

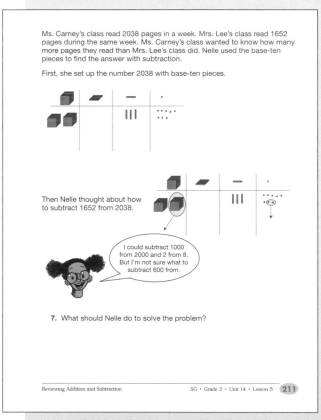

Student Guide - page 211 (Answers on p. 82)

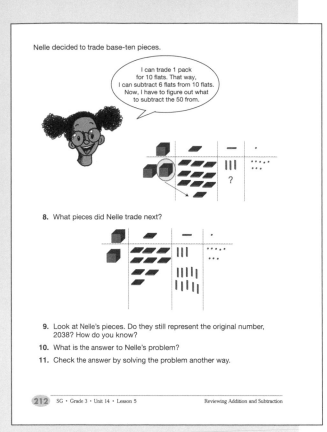

Nelle decided to trade base-ten pieces.

I can trade 1 pack for 10 flats. That way, I can subtract 6 flats from 10 flats. Now, I have to figure out what to subtract the 50 from.

8. What pieces did Nelle trade next?

9. Look at Nelle's pieces. Do they still represent the original number, 2038? How do you know?

10. What is the answer to Nelle's problem?

11. Check the answer by solving the problem another way.

Student Guide - page 212 *(Answers on p. 83)*

Pages and Minutes

Solve Questions 12–15 in two ways. Use paper and pencil and base-ten pieces or base-ten shorthand. Estimate to be sure your answers are reasonable.

12.	4765	13.	803	14.	6409	15.	648
	+ 3829		− 527		− 2576		+ 896

16. Explain a mental math method for Question 13.

17. Explain your estimation strategy for Question 14.

For Questions 18–24, follow these steps:
• Try to say the problem in your own words.
• Solve the problem. You may use paper and pencil, base-ten pieces, or mental math.
• Be sure to write a number sentence for the problem.
• Look back. Does your answer make sense?

18. Ms. Carney's class read 226 pages on Thursday and 284 pages on Friday.
    A. How many pages did the class read on both days?
    B. How many more pages did the class read on Friday than on Thursday?

19. Ms. Carney's class read for 905 minutes on Saturday and for 715 minutes on Sunday. How many more minutes did the class read on Saturday?

20. On Wednesday Ms. Carney's class read for 600 minutes. How many hours is this?

21. A. The class read 210 pages on Monday, 151 pages on Tuesday, and 190 pages on Wednesday. What was the total number of pages read from Monday through Wednesday?
    B. On Thursday the class read 245 pages, and on Friday the class read 177 pages. What was the total number of pages the class read on Thursday and Friday together?
    C. How many pages did the class read in the entire week?

Student Guide - page 213 *(Answers on p. 83)*

The final example displays a subtraction problem in which students must regroup base-ten pieces. As students regroup, remind them that the total value of the pieces should not change. ***Question 9*** reminds students to check the value of the base-ten pieces to be sure the value has not changed after all the trading is completed. However, you may wish to ask students what numbers the pieces represent as each trade is made. See Figure 7.

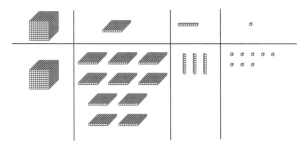

2000 + 0 + 30 + 8 = 2038

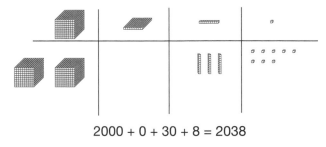

1000 + 1000 + 30 + 8 = 2038

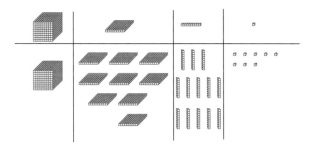

1000 + 900 + 130 + 8 = 2038

Figure 7: *The value of the base-ten pieces as trades are made*

After the class discusses all the examples, students can begin working on the problems in the Pages and Minutes section. These problems use the context of the *Tracking Our Reading* data (Lesson 3) to provide practice in multidigit addition and subtraction. Students can choose from a variety of strategies to solve the problems: They may use base-ten pieces, paper and pencil, or mental math.

Students will probably need to use paper and pencil or manipulatives to solve many of the problems in the Pages and Minutes section. However, students can use a counting-up strategy to answer *Question 22* (1500 – 1301) in their heads. Have students share their solutions with the rest of the class.

Questions 25 and *26* provide a structure for students to use data from the *Tracking Our Reading* class data table to make up their own problems. Students may need help choosing appropriate data for the problems. When they finish, students can trade and solve each other's problems. Or you can make up a worksheet with the best problems and distribute them to the class. More addition and subtraction practice is provided in the Homework section on the *Reviewing Addition and Subtraction* Activity Pages.

Journal Prompt

Make up a problem using data from the class data table for *Tracking Our Reading*.

---

22. Mr. Rodriguez's class is trying to read 1500 pages in one week. They have read 1301 pages so far. How many more pages will they have to read to meet their goal?

23. Mrs. Lee's class is trying to read 1500 pages also. They have read 1158 pages so far. How many more pages do they need to read to meet the goal?

24. **A.** How many more pages had Mr. Rodriguez's class read than Mrs. Lee's class?
    B. How many pages have Mr. Rodriguez's class and Mrs. Lee's class read altogether?

For Questions 25 and 26, you will need to use data from your class data table. Copy each problem on your paper. Fill in the blanks with data from your class data table. Then solve the problems.

25. We read _____ pages on _____ and _____ pages on _____. How many pages did we read on both days?

26. We read for _____ minutes on _____ and for _____ minutes on _____. How many more minutes did we read on _____ than _____?

 Homework

1. Add 478 to each number below. Before you add, estimate each answer.
   A. 25   **B.** 319   **C.** 2035

2. Subtract 478 from each number below. Estimate each answer before you subtract.
   A. 869   **B.** 1227   **C.** 1500

Solve the problem for Questions 3–6. Estimate to be sure your answer is reasonable.

3. At Lucero School, there are 129 students in third grade, 138 students in fourth grade, and 144 students in fifth grade. How many students are in the three grades?

Student Guide - page 214 (Answers on p. 84)

---

4. At King School, there are 1047 students. There are 877 students at Lucero School.
   A. How many students go to these two schools?
   B. How many more students go to King School than Lucero School?
   C. Explain your estimation strategy for Question 4A.
   D. Explain a method for Question 4B using mental math.

5. Lucero School bought 1000 folders so that each student could be given one on the first day of school. How many folders will they have left over?

6. The principal at Lucero School figured out that the school needs 7029 textbooks for all the grades. Right now, the school has 5634 textbooks. How many more textbooks does the principal need to order?

For Questions 7–10, solve each problem in two ways. You may use mental math, paper and pencil, or base-ten shorthand. Estimate to be sure your answers are reasonable.

7.	1530	8.	296	9.	6376	10.	7102
	+ 3492		– 178		– 4584		+ 4367

Student Guide - page 215 (Answers on p. 84)

Homework and Practice

- Assign the Homework section on the *Reviewing Addition and Subtraction* Activity Pages in the *Student Guide*.

- In DPP Bits K and M students compile the class reading data for Lesson 3. Task L builds number sense for fractions by skip counting backwards by thirds. Challenge N is addition and subtraction computation practice.

Assessment

- Use the *Addition and Subtraction* Assessment Blackline Master to assess whether students can solve multidigit addition and subtraction problems using pencil and paper.

- Use the *Observational Assessment Record* to note students' abilities to represent addition and subtraction using base-ten pieces.

- Transfer appropriate documentation from the Unit 14 *Observational Assessment Record* to students' *Individual Assessment Record Sheets*.

Math Facts and Daily Practice and Problems

For DPP Bits K and M, students compile class reading data. Task L involves skip counting with fractions. Challenge N is computation practice.

Teaching the Activity

1. Discuss the examples of students solving multidigit addition and subtraction problems on the *Reviewing Addition and Subtraction* Activity Pages in the *Student Guide.*
2. Students answer *Questions 1–11* by working through the examples using base-ten pieces.
3. Students complete *Questions 12–26* in the Pages and Minutes section on the *Reviewing Addition and Subtraction* Activity Pages.
4. Students may use base-ten pieces, pencil and paper, mental math, or other strategies to solve the problems.
5. Students share their solutions with the class.
6. For *Questions 25* and *26* in the Pages and Minutes section, students use the *Tracking Our Reading* data begun in Lesson 3 to make up addition and subtraction problems.
7. Students trade and solve each other's problems.

Homework

Assign the Homework section on the *Reviewing Addition and Subtraction* Activity Pages.

Assessment

1. Students complete the *Addition and Subtraction* Assessment Blackline Master.
2. Use the *Observational Assessment Record* to note students' abilities to represent multidigit addition and subtraction problems using base-ten pieces.
3. Transfer appropriate documentation from the Unit 14 *Observational Assessment Record* to students' *Individual Assessment Record Sheets.*

Answer Key is on pages 82–85.

Notes:

Addition and Subtraction

Solve each of the following problems. Estimate to be sure your answers are reasonable.

1. 4393
    $+ 7408$

2.   504
    $- 375$

3. 5039
    $- 3657$

4. Explain your estimation strategy for Question 1.

5. Explain a method for solving Question 2 using mental math.

Assessment Blackline Master

6. There are 365 days in a year. How many days are there in two years?

7. Joey read two pages in an encyclopedia. The first page had 1028 words on it. The second page had a picture and 756 words on it.

A. How many fewer words are on the second page than the first?

B. How many words are on the two pages?

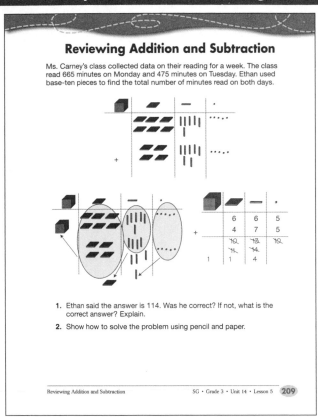

Student Guide - page 209

Student Guide (pp. 209–211)

1. No; 1140; Ethan forgot the zero in the bits column.

2. Possible paper-and-pencil strategy:

   $$\begin{array}{r} \overset{1\ 1}{665} \\ +\ 475 \\ \hline 1140 \end{array}$$

3. 236; yes; explanations will vary. 89 is close to 100; if 100 were added to 147 the answer would be 247. 236 is close to 247.

4. He traded in 10 skinnies for 1 pack and 10 bits for 1 skinny.

5. One stands for a 100 and the other stands for a 10.

6. Answers will vary.

7. She should trade 1 pack for 10 flats.

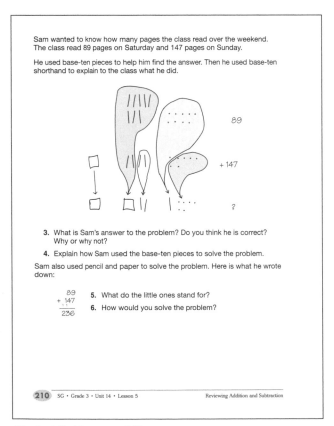

Student Guide - page 210

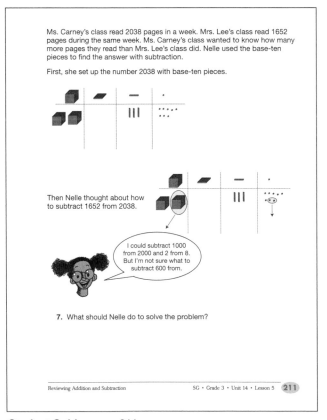

Student Guide - page 211

Student Guide (p. 212)

8. She traded a flat for 10 skinnies. This way she could subtract 50 or 5 skinnies.

9. Yes; $1000 + 900 + 130 + 8 = 2038$

10. 386 pages

11. Strategies will vary. Count up: from 1652 to 2000 is 348 (1650 to 2000 is 350); $348 + 38 = 386$

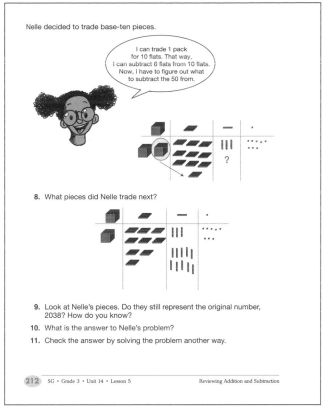

Nelle decided to trade base-ten pieces.

I can trade 1 pack for 10 flats. That way, I can subtract 6 flats from 10 flats. Now, I have to figure out what to subtract the 50 from.

8. What pieces did Nelle trade next?

9. Look at Nelle's pieces. Do they still represent the original number, 2038? How do you know?

10. What is the answer to Nelle's problem?

11. Check the answer by solving the problem another way.

212 SG • Grade 3 • Unit 14 • Lesson 5   Reviewing Addition and Subtraction

Student Guide - page 212

Student Guide (p. 213)

12. 8594

13. 276

14. 3833

15. 1544

16. Possible method: $800 - 525 = 275$; $275 + 3 - 2 = 276$.

17. Possible strategy: $6500 - 2500 = 4000$.

18. A. 510 pages

   B. 58 pages

19. 190 minutes

20. 10 hours

21. A. 551 pages

   B. 422 pages

   C. 973 pages

Pages and Minutes

Solve Questions 12–15 in two ways. Use paper and pencil and base-ten pieces or base-ten shorthand. Estimate to be sure your answers are reasonable.

12. 4765
     + 3829

13.   803
      − 527

14. 6409
     − 2576

15.   648
      + 896

16. Explain a mental math method for Question 13.

17. Explain your estimation strategy for Question 14.

For Questions 18–24, follow these steps:
- Try to say the problem in your own words.
- Solve the problem. You may use paper and pencil, base-ten pieces, or mental math.
- Be sure to write a number sentence for the problem.
- Look back. Does your answer make sense?

18. Ms. Carney's class read 226 pages on Thursday and 284 pages on Friday.
   A. How many pages did the class read on both days?
   B. How many more pages did the class read on Friday than on Thursday?

19. Ms. Carney's class read for 905 minutes on Saturday and for 715 minutes on Sunday. How many more minutes did the class read on Saturday?

20. On Wednesday Ms. Carney's class read for 600 minutes. How many hours is this?

21. A. The class read 210 pages on Monday, 151 pages on Tuesday, and 190 pages on Wednesday. What was the total number of pages read from Monday through Wednesday?
   B. On Thursday the class read 245 pages, and on Friday the class read 177 pages. What was the total number of pages the class read on Thursday and Friday together?
   C. How many pages did the class read in the entire week?

Reviewing Addition and Subtraction   SG • Grade 3 • Unit 14 • Lesson 5 213

Student Guide - page 213

22. Mr. Rodriguez's class is trying to read 1500 pages in one week. They have read 1301 pages so far. How many more pages will they have to read to meet their goal?

23. Mrs. Lee's class is trying to read 1500 pages also. They have read 1158 pages so far. How many more pages do they need to read to meet the goal?

24. A. How many more pages had Mr. Rodriguez's class read than Mrs. Lee's class?

    B. How many pages have Mr. Rodriguez's class and Mrs. Lee's class read altogether?

For Questions 25 and 26, you will need to use data from your class data table. Copy each problem on your paper. Fill in the blanks with data from your class data table. Then solve the problems.

25. We read _____ pages on _____ and _____ pages on _____. How many pages did we read on both days?

26. We read for _____ minutes on _____ and for _____ minutes on _____. How many more minutes did we read on _____ than _____?

Homework

1. Add 478 to each number below. Before you add, estimate each answer.
   A. 25   B. 319   C. 2035

2. Subtract 478 from each number below. Estimate each answer before you subtract.
   A. 869   B. 1227   C. 1500

Solve the problem for Questions 3–6. Estimate to be sure your answer is reasonable.

3. At Lucero School, there are 129 students in third grade, 138 students in fourth grade, and 144 students in fifth grade. How many students are in the three grades?

214 SG • Grade 3 • Unit 14 • Lesson 5   Reviewing Addition and Subtraction

Student Guide - page 214

Student Guide (p. 214)

22. 199 pages

23. 342 pages

24. A. 143 pages

    B. 2459 pages

25.–26. Answers will vary.

Homework

1. A. Estimate = 500; 503

   B. Estimate = 800; 797

   C. Estimate = 2500; 2513

2. A. Estimate = 400; 391

   B. Estimate = 700–750; 749

   C. Estimate = 1000; 1022

3. 411 students

---

4. At King School, there are 1047 students. There are 877 students at Lucero School.
   A. How many students go to these two schools?
   B. How many more students go to King School than Lucero School?
   C. Explain your estimation strategy for Question 4A.
   D. Explain a method for Question 4B using mental math.

5. Lucero School bought 1000 folders so that each student could be given one on the first day of school. How many folders will they have left over?

6. The principal at Lucero School figured out that the school needs 7029 textbooks for all the grades. Right now, the school has 5634 textbooks. How many more textbooks does the principal need to order?

For Questions 7–10, solve each problem in two ways. You may use mental math, paper and pencil, or base-ten shorthand. Estimate to be sure your answers are reasonable.

7. 1530   8. 296   9. 6376   10. 7102
   + 3492   − 178   − 4584   + 4367

Reviewing Addition and Subtraction   SG • Grade 3 • Unit 14 • Lesson 5 215

Student Guide - page 215

Student Guide (p. 215)

4. A. 1924 students

   B. 170 students

   C. Possible strategy: 1000 + 900 = 1900

   D. Possible method: Count up 30 to 907, 100 to 1007, and 40 to 1047.
      30 + 40 + 100 = 170.

5. 1000 − 877 = 123 folders

6. 7029 − 5634 = 1395 textbooks

7. 5022

8. 118

9. 1792

10. 11,469

Unit Resource Guide (p. 80)

Addition and Subtraction

1. 11,801

2. 129

3. 1382

4. Possible strategy: $4400 + 7400 = 11,800$

5. Possible method: Count up: 25 to 400, 100 to 500, and 4 more to 504. $25 + 100 + 4 = 129$.

Name _____ Date _____

Addition and Subtraction

Solve each of the following problems. Estimate to be sure your answers are reasonable.

1. 4393
    $+ 7408$

2. 504
    $- 375$

3. 5039
    $- 3657$

4. Explain your estimation strategy for Question 1.

5. Explain a method for solving Question 2 using mental math.

80   URG • Grade 3 • Unit 14 • Lesson 5   Assessment Blackline Master

Unit Resource Guide - page 80

Unit Resource Guide (p. 81)

6. $365 + 365 = 730$ days

7. **A.** $1028 - 756 = 272$ words

   B. $1028 + 756 = 1784$ words

Name _____ Date _____

6. There are 365 days in a year. How many days are there in two years?

7. Joey read two pages in an encyclopedia. The first page had 1028 words on it. The second page had a picture and 756 words on it.

   A. How many fewer words are on the second page than the first?

   B. How many words are on the two pages?

Assessment Blackline Master   URG • Grade 3 • Unit 14 • Lesson 5   81

Unit Resource Guide - page 81

<table>
<tr><td>

Name _____ Date _____

Unit 14 Home Practice

PART 1
1. 82 + 69 = _____
2. 472 + 579 = _____
3. 8 × 200 = _____
4. 300 × 5 = _____
5. Find two 2-digit numbers with a sum of 137. _____ and _____
6. The normal temperature for July in Nome, Alaska, is 51°F. In Phoenix, Arizona, it is 92°F.
   A. Usually, how many degrees warmer is it in Phoenix than in Nome for the month of July? _____
   B. What is the normal temperature in San Francisco, California, for July if it is 13 degrees warmer than the normal temperature in Nome? _____
   C. What is the normal temperature in San Antonio, Texas, for July if it is 44 degrees warmer than Nome? _____

PART 2
1. 665 − 456 = _____
2. 604 − 456 = _____
3. 350 + 50 + _____ = 1000
4. 1000 − 350 = _____
5. 250 + 400 + _____ = 1000
6. 1000 − 250 = _____
7. 420 + 100 + _____ = 1000
8. 1000 − 420 = _____
9. Nick's family had to drive 143 miles to visit his grandma for Thanksgiving. Nick asked, "Are we there yet?" His dad said, "We have about 47 miles to go." About how many miles had they driven already?

_____

216 DAB • Grade 3 • Unit 14   COLLECTING AND USING DATA

</td></tr>
</table>

Discovery Assignment Book - page 216

Discovery Assignment Book (p. 216)

Part 1
1. 151
2. 1051
3. 1600
4. 1500
5. Answers will vary. 89 and 48, 99 and 38
6. A. 41 degrees
   B. 64 degrees
   C. 95 degrees

Part 2
1. 209
2. 148
3. 600
4. 650
5. 350
6. 750
7. 480
8. 580
9. 96 miles

<table>
<tr><td>

Name _____ Date _____

PART 3
1. How many hops, starting at 0, will it take a +9 mathhopper to pass 80? _____ What number will it land on? _____
2. Measure the perimeter of the rectangle below to the nearest half of a centimeter. _____

[rectangle]

3. How many rectangles are in the figure below? _____

[figure]

PART 4
1. How many 30-minute periods are there from 3:00 P.M. until 10:00 P.M.?

_____

2. Nine hundred fifty-two is . . .
   A. 100 more than _____
   B. 50 more than _____
   C. 50 less than _____
   D. about twice _____
3. Find one way that you can divide five $100 bills, eight $50 bills, and five $20 bills into two equal shares.

_____

COLLECTING AND USING DATA   DAB • Grade 3 • Unit 14 **217**

</td></tr>
</table>

Discovery Assignment Book - page 217

Discovery Assignment Book (p. 217)

Part 3
1. 9 hops; 81
2. 18 cm (7 cm + 2 cm + 7 cm + 2 cm)
3. 9

Part 4
1. 14
2. A. 852
   B. 902
   C. 1002
   D. Answers will vary. 450–500
3. Answers will vary. One possible way to divide is: One person gets the five $100 bills. The other person gets the $50 bills and the $20 bills.

*Answers and/or discussion are included in the Lesson Guide.

Glossary

This glossary provides definitions of key vocabulary terms in the Grade 3 lessons. Locations of key vocabulary terms in the curriculum are included with each definition. Components Key: URG = *Unit Resource Guide*, SG = *Student Guide*, and DAB = *Discovery Assignment Book*.

A

Area (URG Unit 5; SG Unit 5)
The area of a shape is the amount of space it covers, measured in square units.

Array (URG Unit 7 & Unit 11)
An array is an arrangement of elements into a rectangular pattern of (horizontal) rows and (vertical) columns. (*See* column and row.)

Associative Property of Addition (URG Unit 2)
For any three numbers *a, b,* and *c* we have $a + (b + c) = (a + b) + c$. For example in finding the sum of 4, 8, and 2, one can compute $4 + 8$ first and then add 2: $(4 + 8) + 2 = 14$. Alternatively, we can compute $8 + 2$ and then add the result to 4: $4 + (8 + 2) = 4 + 10 = 14$.

Average (URG Unit 5)
A number that can be used to represent a typical value in a set of data. (*See also* mean and median.)

Axes (URG Unit 8; SG Unit 8)
Reference lines on a graph. In the Cartesian coordinate system, the axes are two perpendicular lines that meet at the origin. The singular of axes is axis.

B

Base (of a cube model) (URG Unit 18; SG Unit 18)
The part of a cube model that sits on the "ground."

Base-Ten Board (URG Unit 4)
A tool to help children organize base-ten pieces when they are representing numbers.

Base-Ten Pieces (URG Unit 4; SG Unit 4)
A set of manipulatives used to model our number system as shown in the figure at the right. Note that a skinny is made of 10 bits, a flat is made of 100 bits, and a pack is made of 1000 bits.

Base-Ten Shorthand (SG Unit 4)
A pictorial representation of the base-ten pieces as shown.

Nickname	Picture	Shorthand
bit	⬜	•
skinny	▭▭▭▭	/
flat	▱	⬭
pack	⬛	⬭

Best-Fit Line (URG Unit 9; SG Unit 9; DAB Unit 9)
The line that comes closest to the most number of points on a point graph.

Bit (URG Unit 4; SG Unit 4)
A cube that measures 1 cm on each edge. It is the smallest of the base-ten pieces that is often used to represent 1. (*See also* base-ten pieces.)

C

Capacity (URG Unit 16)
1. The volume of the inside of a container.
2. The largest volume a container can hold.

Cartesian Coordinate System (URG Unit 8)
A method of locating points on a flat surface by means of numbers. This method is named after its originator, René Descartes. (*See also* coordinates.)

Centimeter (cm)
A unit of measure in the metric system equal to one-hundredth of a meter. (1 inch = 2.54 cm)

Column (URG Unit 11)
In an array, the objects lined up vertically.

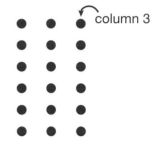
column 3

Common Fraction (URG Unit 15)
Any fraction that is written with a numerator and denominator that are whole numbers. For example, $\frac{3}{4}$ and $\frac{9}{4}$ are both common fractions. (*See also* decimal fraction.)

Commutative Property of Addition (URG Unit 2 & Unit 11)
This is also known as the Order Property of Addition. Changing the order of the addends does not change the sum. For example, $3 + 5 = 5 + 3 = 8$. Using variables, $n + m = m + n$.

Commutative Property of Multiplication (URG Unit 11)
Changing the order of the factors in a multiplication problem does not change the result, e.g., $7 \times 3 = 3 \times 7 = 21$. (*See also* turn-around facts.)

Congruent (URG Unit 12 & Unit 17; SG Unit 12)
Figures with the same shape and size.

Convenient Number (URG Unit 6)
A number used in computation that is close enough to give a good estimate, but is also easy to compute mentally, e.g., 25 and 30 are convenient numbers for 27.

Coordinates (URG Unit 8; SG Unit 8)
An ordered pair of numbers that locates points on a flat surface by giving distances from a pair of coordinate axes. For example, if a point has coordinates (4, 5) it is 4 units from the vertical axis and 5 units from the horizontal axis.

Counting Back (URG Unit 2)
A strategy for subtracting in which students start from a larger number and then count down until the number is reached. For example, to solve $8 - 3$, begin with 8 and count down three, 7, 6, 5.

Counting Down (*See* counting back.)

Counting Up (URG Unit 2)
A strategy for subtraction in which the student starts at the lower number and counts on to the higher number. For example, to solve $8 - 5$, the student starts at 5 and counts up three numbers (6, 7, 8). So $8 - 5 = 3$.

Cube (SG Unit 18)
A three-dimensional shape with six congruent square faces.

Cubic Centimeter (cc) (URG Unit 16; SG Unit 16)
The volume of a cube that is one centimeter long on each edge.

1 cm
1 cm
1 cm
cubic centimeter

Cup (URG Unit 16)
A unit of volume equal to 8 fluid ounces, one-half pint.

D

Decimal Fraction (URG Unit 15)
A fraction written as a decimal. For example, 0.75 and 0.4 are decimal fractions and $\frac{75}{100}$ and $\frac{4}{10}$ are called common fractions. (*See also* fraction.)

Denominator (URG Unit 13)
The number below the line in a fraction. The denominator indicates the number of equal parts in which the unit whole is divided. For example, the 5 is the denominator in the fraction $\frac{2}{5}$. In this case the unit whole is divided into five equal parts.

Density (URG Unit 16)
The ratio of an object's mass to its volume.

Difference (URG Unit 2)
The answer to a subtraction problem.

Dissection (URG Unit 12 & Unit 17)
Cutting or decomposing a geometric shape into smaller shapes that cover it exactly.

Distributive Property of Multiplication over Addition (URG Unit 19)
For any three numbers a, b, and c, $a \times (b + c) = a \times b + a \times c$. The distributive property is the foundation for most methods of multidigit multiplication. For example, $9 \times (17) = 9 \times (10 + 7) = 9 \times 10 + 9 \times 7 = 90 + 63 = 153$.

E

Equal-Arm Balance
See two-pan balance.

Equilateral Triangle (URG Unit 7)
A triangle with all sides of equal length and all angles of equal measure.

Equivalent Fractions (SG Unit 17)
Fractions that have the same value, e.g., $\frac{2}{4} = \frac{1}{2}$.

Estimate (URG Unit 5 & Unit 6)
1. (verb) To find *about* how many.
2. (noun) An approximate number.

Extrapolation (URG Unit 7)
Using patterns in data to make predictions or to estimate values that lie beyond the range of values in the set of data.

F

Fact Family (URG Unit 11; SG Unit 11)
Related math facts, e.g., $3 \times 4 = 12$, $4 \times 3 = 12$, $12 \div 3 = 4$, $12 \div 4 = 3$.

Factor (URG Unit 11; SG Unit 11)
1. In a multiplication problem, the numbers that are multiplied together. In the problem $3 \times 4 = 12$, 3 and 4 are the factors.
2. Whole numbers that can be multiplied together to get a number. That is, numbers that divide a number evenly, e.g., 1, 2, 3, 4, 6, and 12 are all the factors of 12.

Fewest Pieces Rule (URG Unit 4 & Unit 6; SG Unit 4)
Using the least number of base-ten pieces to represent a number. (*See also* base-ten pieces.)

Flat (URG Unit 4; SG Unit 4)
A block that measures 1 cm $\times$ 10 cm $\times$ 10 cm. It is one of the base-ten pieces that is often used to represent 100. (*See also* base-ten pieces.)

Flip (URG Unit 12)
A motion of the plane in which a figure is reflected over a line so that any point and its image are the same distance from the line.

Fraction (URG Unit 15)
A number that can be written as $\frac{a}{b}$ where a and b are whole numbers and b is not zero. For example, $\frac{1}{2}$, 0.5, and 2 are all fractions since 0.5 can be written as $\frac{5}{10}$ and 2 can be written as $\frac{2}{1}$.

Front-End Estimation (URG Unit 6)
Estimation by looking at the left-most digit.

G

Gallon (gal) (URG Unit 16)
A unit of volume equal to four quarts.

Gram
The basic unit used to measure mass.

H

Hexagon (SG Unit 12)
A six-sided polygon.

Horizontal Axis (SG Unit 1)
In a coordinate grid, the x-axis. The axis that extends from left to right.

I

Interpolation (URG Unit 7)
Making predictions or estimating values that lie between data points in a set of data.

J

K

Kilogram
1000 grams.

L

Likely Event (SG Unit 1)
An event that has a high probability of occurring.

Line of Symmetry (URG Unit 12)
A line is a line of symmetry for a plane figure if, when the figure is folded along this line, the two parts match exactly.

Line Symmetry (URG Unit 12; SG Unit 12)
A figure has line symmetry if it has at least one line of symmetry.

Liter (l) (URG Unit 16; SG Unit 16)
Metric unit used to measure volume. A liter is a little more than a quart.

M

Magic Square (URG Unit 2)
A square array of digits in which the sums of the rows, columns, and main diagonals are the same.

Making a Ten (URG Unit 2)
Strategies for addition and subtraction that make use of knowing the sums to ten. For example, knowing $6 + 4 = 10$ can be helpful in finding $10 - 6 = 4$ and $11 - 6 = 5$.

Mass (URG Unit 9 & Unit 16; SG Unit 9)
The amount of matter in an object.

Mean (URG Unit 5)
An average of a set of numbers that is found by adding the values of the data and dividing by the number of values.

Measurement Division (URG Unit 7)
Division as equal grouping. The total number of objects and the number of objects in each group are known. The number of groups is the unknown. For example, tulip bulbs come in packages of 8. If 216 bulbs are sold, how many packages are sold?

Measurement Error (URG Unit 9)
The unavoidable error that occurs due to the limitations inherent to any measurement instrument.

Median (URG Unit 5; DAB Unit 5)
For a set with an odd number of data arranged in order, it is the middle number. For an even number of data arranged in order, it is the number halfway between the two middle numbers.

Meniscus (URG Unit 16; SG Unit 16)
The curved surface formed when a liquid creeps up the side of a container (for example, a graduated cylinder).

Meter (m)
The standard unit of length measure in the metric system. One meter is approximately 39 inches.

Milliliter (ml) (URG Unit 16; SG Unit 16)
A measure of capacity in the metric system that is the volume of a cube that is one centimeter long on each edge.

Multiple (URG Unit 3 & Unit 11)
A number is a multiple of another number if it is evenly divisible by that number. For example, 12 is a multiple of 2 since 2 divides 12 evenly.

N

Numerator (URG Unit 13)
The number written above the line in a fraction. For example, the 2 is the numerator in the fraction $\frac{2}{5}$. (*See also* denominator.)

O

One-Dimensional Object (URG Unit 18; SG Unit 18)
An object is one-dimensional if it is made up of pieces of lines and curves.

Ordered Pairs (URG Unit 8)
A pair of numbers that gives the coordinates of a point on a grid in relation to the origin. The horizontal coordinate is given first; the vertical coordinate is given second. For example, the ordered pair (5, 3) tells us to move five units to the right of the origin and 3 units up.

Origin (URG Unit 8)
The point at which the *x*- and *y*-axes (horizontal and vertical axes) intersect on a coordinate plane. The origin is described by the ordered pair (0, 0) and serves as a reference point so that all the points on the plane can be located by ordered pairs.

P

Pack (URG Unit 4; SG Unit 4)
A cube that measures 10 cm on each edge. It is one of the base-ten pieces that is often used to represent 1000. (*See also* base-ten pieces.)

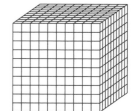

Palindrome (URG Unit 6)
A number, word, or phrase that reads the same forward and backward, e.g., 12321.

Parallel Lines (URG Unit 18)
Lines that are in the same direction. In the plane, parallel lines are lines that do not intersect.

Parallelogram (URG Unit 18)
A quadrilateral with two pairs of parallel sides.

Partitive Division (URG Unit 7)
Division as equal sharing. The total number of objects and the number of groups are known. The number of objects in each group is the unknown. For example, Frank has 144 marbles that he divides equally into 6 groups. How many marbles are in each group?

Pentagon (SG Unit 12)
A five-sided, five-angled polygon.

Perimeter (URG Unit 7; DAB Unit 7)
The distance around a two-dimensional shape.

Pint (URG Unit 16)
A unit of volume measure equal to 16 fluid ounces, i.e., two cups.

Polygon
A two-dimensional connected figure made of line segments in which each endpoint of every side meets with an endpoint of exactly one other side.

Population (URG Unit 1; SG Unit 1)
A collection of persons or things whose properties will be analyzed in a survey or experiment.

Prediction (SG Unit 1)
Using data to declare or foretell what is likely to occur.

Prime Number (URG Unit 11)
A number that has exactly two factors. For example, 7 has exactly two distinct factors, 1 and 7.

Prism
A three-dimensional figure that has two congruent faces, called bases, that are parallel to each other, and all other faces are parallelograms.

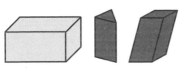

Prisms   Not a prism

Product (URG Unit 11; SG Unit 11; DAB Unit 11)
The answer to a multiplication problem. In the problem $3 \times 4 = 12$, 12 is the product.

Q

Quadrilateral (URG Unit 18)
A polygon with four sides.

Quart (URG Unit 16)
A unit of volume equal to 32 fluid ounces; one quarter of a gallon.

R

Recording Sheet (URG Unit 4)
A place value chart used for addition and subtraction problems.

Rectangular Prism (URG Unit 18; SG Unit 18)
A prism whose bases are rectangles. A right rectangular prism is a prism having all faces rectangles.

Regular (URG Unit 7; DAB Unit 7)
A polygon is regular if all sides are of equal length and all angles are equal.

Remainder (URG Unit 7)
Something that remains or is left after a division problem. The portion of the dividend that is not evenly divisible by the divisor, e.g., $16 \div 5 = 3$ with 1 as a remainder.

Right Angle (SG Unit 12)
An angle that measures 90°.

Rotation (turn) (URG Unit 12)
A transformation (motion) in which a figure is turned a specified angle and direction around a point.

Row (URG Unit 11)
In an array, the objects lined up horizontally.

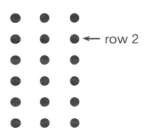

← row 2

Rubric (URG Unit 2)
A written guideline for assigning scores to student work, for the purpose of assessment.

S

Sample (URG Unit 1; SG Unit 1)
A part or subset of a population.

Skinny (URG Unit 4; SG Unit 4)
A block that measures 1 cm × 1 cm × 10 cm. It is one of the base-ten pieces that is often used to represent 10. (*See also* base-ten pieces.)

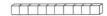

Square Centimeter (sq cm) (SG Unit 5)
The area of a square that is 1 cm long on each side.

Square Number (SG Unit 11)
A number that is the product of a whole number multiplied by itself. For example, 25 is a square number since $5 \times 5 = 25$. A square number can be represented by a square array with the same number of rows as columns. A square array for 25 has 5 rows of 5 objects in each row or 25 total objects.

Standard Masses
A set of objects with convenient masses, usually 1 g, 10 g, 100 g, etc.

Sum (URG Unit 2; SG Unit 2)
The answer to an addition problem.

Survey (URG Unit 14; SG Unit 14)
An investigation conducted by collecting data from a sample of a population and then analyzing it. Usually surveys are used to make predictions about the entire population.

T

Tangrams (SG Unit 12)
A type of geometric puzzle. A shape is given and it must be covered exactly with seven standard shapes called tans.

Thinking Addition (URG Unit 2)
A strategy for subtraction that uses a related addition problem. For example, $15 - 7 = 8$ because $8 + 7 = 15$.

Three-Dimensional (URG Unit 18; SG Unit 18)
Existing in three-dimensional space; having length, width, and depth.

TIMS Laboratory Method (URG Unit 1; SG Unit 1)
A method that students use to organize experiments and investigations. It involves four components: draw, collect, graph, and explore. It is a way to help students learn about the scientific method.

Turn (URG Unit 12)
(*See* rotation.)

Turn-Around Facts (URG Unit 2 & Unit 11 p. 37; SG Unit 11)
Addition facts that have the same addends but in a different order, e.g., $3 + 4 = 7$ and $4 + 3 = 7$. (*See also* commutative property of addition and commutative property of multiplication.)

Two-Dimensional (URG Unit 18; SG Unit 18)
Existing in the plane; having length and width.

Two-Pan Balance
A device for measuring the mass of an object by balancing the object against a number of standard masses (usually multiples of 1 unit, 10 units, and 100 units, etc.).

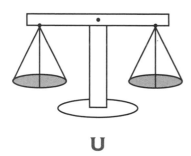

U

Unit (of measurement) (URG Unit 18)
A precisely fixed quantity used to measure. For example, centimeter, foot, kilogram, and quart are units of measurement.

Using a Ten (URG Unit 2)
1. A strategy for addition that uses partitions of the number 10. For example, one can find $8 + 6$ by thinking $8 + 6 = 8 + 2 + 4 = 10 + 4 = 14$.
2. A strategy for subtraction that uses facts that involve subtracting 10. For example, students can use $17 - 10 = 7$ to learn the "close fact" $17 - 9 = 8$.

Using Doubles (URG Unit 2)
Strategies for addition and subtraction that use knowing doubles. For example, one can find $7 + 8$ by thinking $7 + 8 = 7 + 7 + 1 = 14 + 1 = 15$. Knowing $7 + 7 = 14$ can be helpful in finding $14 - 7 = 7$ and $14 - 8 = 6$.

V

Value (URG Unit 1; SG Unit 1)
The possible outcomes of a variable. For example, red, green, and blue are possible values for the variable *color*. Two meters and 1.65 meters are possible values for the variable *length*.

Variable (URG Unit 1; SG Unit 1)
1. An attribute or quantity that changes or varies.
2. A symbol that can stand for a variable.

Vertex (URG Unit 12; SG Unit 12)
1. A point where the sides of a polygon meet.
2. A point where the edges of a three-dimensional object meet.

Vertical Axis (SG Unit 1)
In a coordinate grid, the *y*-axis. It is perpendicular to the horizontal axis.

Volume (URG Unit 16; SG Unit 16)
The measure of the amount of space occupied by an object.

Volume by Displacement (URG Unit 16)
A way of measuring volume of an object by measuring the amount of water (or some other fluid) it displaces.

W

Weight (URG Unit 9)
A measure of the pull of gravity on an object. One unit for measuring weight is the pound.

X

Y

Z